LAUGHING, LOVING, LIVING YOUR WAY TO A STRESS-FREE *life*

Dr. Jeffrey M. Smith, D.C.

good life press.

LAUGHING, LOVING, LIVING YOUR WAY TO A STRESS-FREE *life*

Copyright © 2008 Good Life Press.

All rights reserved. No part of this book may be reproduced in any form or by any means, without permission in writing from the publisher.

Printed in the United States of America
10 9 8 7 6 5 4 3 2 1

ISBN: 978-0-9792679-0-1

> Good Life Press & Dr. Jeffrey Smith
> www.drjeffreysmith.com
> 7716 W. North Ave.
> Elmwood Park, IL 60707
> funnydr@aol.com
> Office contact number: 708-456-8844

Yoga clip art © Iyengar Yoga Institute of San Francisco.

DISCLAIMER

This book and the advice given are not intended to take the place of your physician. I recommend all patients consult with their primary care physician before following any of the advice in this book.

ABOUT
DR. JEFFREY M. SMITH

As a practicing Chiropractic physician and lecturer since 1979, Dr. Smith helps over 500 new patients per year regain their health. Dr. Smith has successfully treated over 25,000 people for aches and pains due to stress and is committed to improving the lives of as many people as possible.

Dr. Smith was born in Hartford, Connecticut and received his primary and secondary education in Connecticut and New York. While completing his undergraduate at the Southern and Central Connecticut State Colleges, he was employed at the Yale University School of Medicine. He then moved to Illinois and enrolled in National College of Chiropractic in Lombard, where he received a Bachelor of Science in Human Biology. There, he also obtained his Doctor of Chiropractic degree, a seven-year program. He interned at Chicago General Health Services in 1970.

As a member of many associations such as, the Professional Speakers of Illinois, the National Speakers Association, the American Heart Association and the American Association for Therapeutic Humor. He has trained at The Second City in Chicago for improvisational speaking, where he developed his speaking style. He has given hundreds of presentations on healthful living at businesses (Colombia College, U.S. Cellular, Marriot and others) and taught health and wellness to dozens of fire departments in the greater Chicago area. He has spoken at over

300 schools to teachers about stress and health and treated over 1,500 teachers. He is an instructor at Triton College and the Cook County Sheriff Police academy.

Dr. Smith resides just west of Chicago and has four wonderful children: David, Alicia, Mariah and Jacob.

ACKNOWLEDGMENTS

Since 1988 Martin Sage has been a constant inspiration to me. His coaching, workshops and friendship not only allowed me to write this book but have guided me to be, "All that I can be". For that I am eternally grateful.

To Ron Louis, the main man behind this book.

And of course, to the wonderful and beautiful Dr. Carly M. Smith

PLANNING A CONFERENCE?

Dr. Smith is considered an expert on health, productivity, humor and preventing burnout. His presentations are entertaining, informative and really good.

www.drjeffreysmith.com
7716 W. North Ave.
Elmwood Park, IL 60707
funnydr@aol.com
Office contact number: 708-456-8844

DEDICATIONS

To the beacon of light, in the window of life,

I dedicate this book:

To Carly, David, Alicia, Mariah, & Jacob

In loving memory of my mother, Irene Francis

and Amanda Ashley Smith.

May they rest in peace.

TABLE OF CONTENTS

Introduction	**xi**
CHAPTER ONE How Stress Can Make you Sick and Crazy	**1**
CHAPTER TWO Laughing, Loving, and Living: What You Can Do To Handle or Manage Stress	**33**
CHAPTER THREE The Relaxation Solution: Meditation, Spirituality, Deep Breathing, Calming Your Mind and Chillin'	**75**
CHAPTER FOUR De-Stress with Chiropractic Care	**113**
CHAPTER FIVE The Exercise and Nutrition Solution	**129**
Conclusion	159
Recommended Reading & Resources	161

INTRODUCTION

> "SOMETIMES WHEN PEOPLE ARE UNDER STRESS, THEY HATE TO THINK, AND IT'S THE TIME WHEN THEY MOST NEED TO THINK." — BILL CLINTON, FORMER PRESIDENT OF THE UNITED STATES

Why did the chicken cross the road? He was so stressed out because his girlfriend left him. He couldn't pay his bills and he couldn't lay eggs. So he just had to get away from it all. I know chickens aren't male. Are you going to start hassling me?

Every day, I witness the impact stress has on health when my patients tell me about all the stress in their lives. If you're stressed out, you're not alone. Everyone feels the effects of stress. We all experience it, but most people don't know what to do about stress. No single idea or technique can relieve all of your stress—you'll need to experiment and try various techniques to find the ones that work for you. Effective stress management is something that must become part of your daily life—just like brushing your teeth, eating breakfast or scratching your rear end.

Have you ever noticed often times people we know who majored in psychology have had to wrestle with mental health? Well I've had more than my share of stresses over the years. So I started studying stress management. So much so I've become somewhat of an expert on the subject. Then I've noticed many thousands of my patient's health problems were caused or aggravated by unmanaged stress.

So that is where this book comes in. I've put together what I consider the most useful techniques you can utilize to make yourself healthier and happier.

HOW TO USE THIS BOOK

I recommend that you focus on making small incremental changes in your life instead of setting huge, intimidating goals for yourself. Implement the suggestions in this book over weeks or even months. Remember, small changes can add up to big changes. I'm a big proponent of taking on big projects by breaking them down into their smallest tasks and chipping away at them over time. It simply isn't possible for anyone to change their life overnight. But if you follow the guidelines and tips I've outlined in this book, you will be amazed at the differences it can make in your life over time and the feeling of wellness that can follow. It's worked for me and thousands of my patients and it can work for you, too. And by the way, thanks for reading my book. Remember just like I say to my kids, you're the best ever.

LAUGHING,
LOVING, LIVING
YOUR WAY TO
A STRESS-FREE
life

CHAPTER ONE

HOW STRESS CAN MAKE YOU SICK AND CRAZY

"REALITY IS THE LEADING CAUSE OF STRESS AMONGST THOSE IN TOUCH WITH IT" —LILY TOMLIN

Bad news, people. Too much stress or unmanaged stress can ruin your life. In fact, stress is one of the most damaging medical conditions of our time. As a chiropractic physician with almost thirty years experience who has treated around 25,000 patients, I've come to believe that stress is an epidemic and that anyone interested in their health and happiness must seriously consider evaluating and treating the stress in their life.

Let's start with the REALLY bad news:

Experts all over the place agree that stress is, well, stressing us out.

Seventy-five percent of the general population experiences at least "some stress" every two weeks (National Health Interview Survey). Research shows that 60% to 90% of doctor visits are stress related (Harvard Business Review, 1994).

Workplace stress costs more than $300 billion each year in health care costs, missed work and stress-reduction treatments (American Institute of Stress).

Stressed-out workers incur health care costs that are 46 percent higher, or an average of $600 more per person, than other employees (Steven L. Sauter, chief of the Organizational Science and Human Factors Branch of the National Institute for Occupational Safety and Health.

Most health problems are linked to stress:

Cancer	Headaches
Heart Disease	Irritable Bowel Syndrome
Strokes	Constipation
High Blood Pressure	Gastrointestinal problems
Diabetes	Sexual Problems
Depression	Anger
Dementia	Road Rage
Obesity	Spousal Abuse
Fatigue	Immune Response Deficiency
Insomnia	
Backaches	Memory loss
Neck pains	Obesity

This is bad news. And in this chapter, we're going to explore what stress is and how it causes problems in our lives, but I promise we'll get to the fun stuff after that.

Why should you need stress defined for you? You're probably experiencing it on a regular basis and that's why you're here reading this book.

Actually, it's important to for us to be on the same page about what exactly stress is and how it manifests itself. "Stress" is such a pervasive catch-all word in today's culture that it's become practically meaningless. You might be surprised to learn that "good" stress exists.

RECOGNIZING STRESS

Question: Which of these scenarios is stressful?

- You receive a promotion at work.
- Your car has a flat tire.
- You go to a fun party that lasts till 2:00 a.m.
- Your dog gets sick.
- Your new bedroom set is being delivered.
- Your best friend and his wife come to stay at your house for a week.
- You get a bad case of hay fever.
- Getting hit in the head with a shovel

Answer: All of these are stressful!

If you are used to thinking that stress is something that makes you worry, you have the wrong idea about stress. Stress can be caused by a range of situations: happy, sad, allergic, competitive, etc. Many people carry enormous stress loads and don't even realize it!

> "BRAIN CELLS CREATE IDEAS. STRESS KILLS BRAIN CELLS.
> STRESS IS NOT A GOOD IDEA." —FREDERICK SAUNDERS

4 WHAT IS STRESS?

We are all familiar with the word "stress." Stress is when you are worried about getting laid off your job, worried about having enough money to pay bills, or worried about your mother when the doctor says she may need an operation. In fact, to most of us, stress is synonymous with worry.

But your body has a much broader definition of stress. TO YOUR BODY, STRESS IS SYNONYMOUS WITH CHANGE. Anything that causes a change in your life causes stress. It doesn't matter if it's a "good" change or a "bad" change, they are both stressors. When you find your dream apartment and get ready to move, that's stress. If you break your leg, that's stress. Good or bad, if a CHANGE happens in your life, that's stress as far as your body is concerned.

Stress is your body's way of responding to any kind of demand. When something going on around you makes you feel stressed, your body reacts by releasing chemicals into the blood. These chemicals pump you up with energy and strength. Of course, this is great if your stress is caused by physical danger: you're focused, you run faster and you can lift more weight. But those chemicals just get in the way if your stress is a response to something emotional because all that extra energy and strength doesn't have an outlet.

> STRESS CAN HAVE A HUGE IMPACT ON EVERY PART OF YOUR BODY.
> IT CAN WRECK HAVOC ON EVERY BODY SYSTEM.

Even IMAGINED CHANGE is stress. Imagining changes is what we call "worrying." If you fear that you will not be able to finish a project on time, that's stress. If you worry about not getting a job you applied for, that's stress. If you think that you may receive a promotion at work, that's also stress—even though this would probably be a good change for you. Whether the event is good or bad, thinking about change in your life is stressful.

> ANYTHING THAT CAUSES
> CHANGE IN YOUR DAILY ROUTINE
> IS STRESSFUL.
>
> ANYTHING THAT CAUSES
> CHANGE IN YOUR BODY'S HEALTH
> IS STRESSFUL.
>
> IMAGINED CHANGES
> ARE JUST AS STRESSFUL AS REAL CHANGES.

The current and most commonly-accepted definition of stress is the condition experienced when a person perceives that the demands he or she faces exceed the personal and social resources the individual is able to muster.

Everyone reacts to stress differently. Everyone has a different stress threshold, and only you can assess your tolerance level to stressful situations. Also, one person's stressor may not faze another person, and visa versa.

The best treatment for stress is to prevent yourself from getting into situations that are likely to overwhelm your ability to cope. Of course, that's not always possible because many stressors are beyond your control.

NOT ALL STRESS IS BAD

According to Hans Selye, who you'll read about later, "Stress is the spice of life." He determined that essentially there are two kinds of stress-- the good kind (eustress), and the bad kind (distress). Good stress can be associated with you meeting a challenge, coming in first or winning, getting a promotion or even riding on a roller coaster. Distress, as you've been reading about, is the kind of stress that will damage your body, your spirit, and can ultimately shorten your life.

TAKE THE STRESS TEST

In the following table, look up representative changes in your life and see how much stress value each of these changes is adding to your life. NOTE ANY ITEM THAT YOU MAY HAVE EXPERIENCED IN THE LAST TWELVE MONTHS. Then, total up your score.

Stress	Event Value
Death of a spouse	100
Divorce	60
Menopause	60
Separation from living partner	60
Jail term or probation	60
Death of close family member other than spouse	60
Serious personal injury or illness	45
Marriage or establishing life partnership	45
Fired at work	45
Marital or relationship reconciliation	40
Retirement	40
Change in health of immediate family member	40
Work more than 40 hours per week	35
Pregnancy or causing pregnancy	35
Sex difficulties	35
Gain of new family member	35
Business or work role change	35
Change in financial state	35

Stress	Event Value
Death of a close friend (not a family member)	30
Change in number of arguments with spouse or life partner	30
Mortgage or loan for a major purpose	25
Foreclosure of mortgage or loan	25
Sleep less than eight hours per night	25
Change in responsibilities at work	25
Trouble with in-laws, or children	25
Outstanding personal achievement	25
Spouse begins or stops work	20
Begin or end school	20
Change in living conditions (visitors in the home, change in roommates, remodeling house)	20
Change in personal habits (diet, exercise, smoking, etc.)	20
Chronic allergies	20
Trouble with boss	20
Change in work hours or conditions	15
Moving to new residence	15
Presently in pre-menstrual period	15
Change in schools	15
Change in religious activities	15
Change in social activities (more or less than before)	15
Minor financial loan	10
Change in frequency of family get-togethers	10
Vacation	10
Presently in winter holiday season	10
Minor violation of the law	5
Total Score	

(Adapted from the "Social Readjustment Rating Scale" by Thomas Holmes and Richard Rahe. This scale was first published in the *Journal of Psychosomatic Research*, © 1967, Vol. II p. 214.)

We have asked you to look at the last twelve months of changes in your life. This may surprise you. It is crucial to understand, however, that a major change in your life has effects that carry over long periods of time. It's like dropping a rock into a pond. After the initial splash, you will experience ripples of stress. And these ripples may continue in your life for at least a year.

So, if you have experienced total stress within the last twelve months of 250 or greater, even with normal stress tolerance, you may be OVERSTRESSED. Persons with Low Stress Tolerance may be OVERSTRESSED at levels as low as 150.

OVERSTRESS will make you sick. Carrying too heavy a stress load is like running your car engine past the red line, leaving your toaster stuck in the "on" position or running a nuclear reactor past the maximum power allowed. Sooner or later, something will break, burn up or melt down.

TOP TEN STRESSFUL LIFE EVENTS

Spouse's death

Divorce

Marriage separation

Jail term

Death of a close relative

Injury or illness

Marriage

Fired from job

Marriage reconciliation

Retirement

Source: Holmes-Rahe Life Stress Inventory

RISK FACTORS FOR STRESS

The presence of a stressor doesn't automatically result in disabling stress symptoms. The degree to which any stressful situation or event impacts your daily functioning depends partly on the nature of the stressor itself and partly on your own personal and external resources.

STRESS: HOW VULNERABLE ARE YOU?

The nature of the stressor	Stressors that involve central aspects of your life (your marriage, your job) or are chronic issues (a physical handicap, living from paycheck to paycheck) are more likely to cause severe distress.
A crisis experience	Sudden, intense crisis situations (being injured, being diagnosed with a life threatening disease, robbed at gunpoint or attacked by a dog) are understandably overwhelming. Without immediate intervention and treatment, debilitating stress symptoms are common.
Multiple stressors or life changes	Stressors are cumulative, so the more life changes or daily hassles you're dealing with at any one time, the more intense the symptoms of stress.
Your perception of the stressor	The same stressor can have very different effects on different people. For example, public speaking stresses many out, but others thrive on it. If you're able to see some benefit to the situation — the silver lining or a hard lesson learned — the stressor is easier to deal with.
Your knowledge and preparation	The more you know about a stressful situation, including how long it will last and what to expect, the better you'll be able to face it.
Your stress tolerance	Some people roll with the punches, while others crumble at the slightest obstacle or frustration. The more confidence you have in yourself and your ability to persevere, the better you'll be able to take a stressful situation in stride. Some of your tolerance is in your DNA, some has to do with your environment during your childhood, especially the first three years of life.
	Were your parents supportive, nurturing and constantly filling you with unconditional love for your first seven years of life? And did you perceive your mother and father (or other adults who were around a lot) as happy during those formative years? This sets your thermostat for life to some degree.
	To a large extent, your dad influenced the left side of your brain, or logical side, which may be seen on the right side of your face. And your mom influenced the right side of your brain seen (the left side of your face, for right handed people). So pick your parents very carefully.

Your support network

A strong network of supportive friends and family members is an incredibly important buffer against life's stressors. The more lonely or isolated you are, the higher your risk of stress. Being lonely also worsens heart disease.

Having someone to love and be loved by can give some people a lot more ability to handle stress. Conversely, being dumped by a loved one can be devastating or heartbreaking and can literally contribute to a heart attack.

It's the "not knowing" that can be more stressful: During World War II in England, the people in villages that were bombed daily experienced less stress than people living in towns that were only occasionally bombed.

"WHAT'S THE DIFFERENCE BETWEEN STRESS, TENSION AND PANIC? STRESS IS WHEN WIFE IS PREGNANT, TENSION IS WHEN GIRLFRIEND IS PREGNANT, AND PANIC IS WHEN BOTH ARE PREGNANT." — UNKNOWN

WHAT CAUSES STRESS?

In this fast-paced world of ours, full of deadlines, internet, cell phones and the push to succeed, what doesn't cause stress?

MONEY:

Not having enough

Feeling pressure to buy things we cannot afford (like a new car)

Credit card debt

General debt

Job loss

A wife who needs a big home (and a big diamond) to be happy

A divorce or two

Family arguments about money

Dealing with inflation

Children (My accountant sent me a box of condoms for Chanukah…)

WORK:

Work would be fine if it weren't for all those other people

Not having a career we like

A jerk of a boss

Meeting deadlines and other time pressures

Returning phone calls

Heavy case or client load

Returning too many emails in one day

Working overtime

Competition

Office politics or tension

Client and/or partner expectations and demands

Generating new clients and/or more business

FAMILY:

Demands on your time and attention

Spousal problems and conflicts

Not having a spouse and wanting one

Dating

Family tensions and conflicts

Satisfying your personal wants and needs (that's right, most people have a so-so sex life)

Dealing with children (I love my children more than anything, but my young son Jacob thought his name was Vasectomy for a long time, because whenever he would misbehave, I would shake my head and say, "Vasectomy." Speaking of a vasectomy, when my ex found out that I was planning to get one, she offered to perform the procedure using a meat cleaver. And she's not even a surgeon.)

DEALING WITH AGING PARENTS

> "MONEY IS NOT THE PROBLEM; IT'S THE LACK OF MONEY THAT GETS US." — UNKNOWN

ILLNESS AND HEALTH

Catching a cold

Not feeling energetic

Back aches

An aging body

Skin infection

Chronic health issues

Pushing your body too hard

Spinal misalignment

> "THERE ARE VERY FEW CERTAINTIES THAT TOUCH US ALL IN THIS MORTAL EXPERIENCE, BUT ONE OF THE ABSOLUTES IS THAT WE WILL EXPERIENCE HARDSHIP AND STRESS AT SOME POINT."
> — DR. JAMES C. DOBSON, AUTHOR AND RADIO BROADCASTER

ENVIRONMENTAL STRESS

Too hot or too cold climates

Seasonal changes

Pollution

High altitude

Air quality

Water quality

Secondhand smoke

OTHER STRESSORS

Population density (crowds, traffic jams)

Loneliness

Noise

Threat or actuality of earthquakes, fires, flooding, riots

Local and global conflicts

Watching the news

> "OUR GREATEST SOURCE OF PLEASURE IS OUR GREATEST
> SOURCE OF POTENTIAL STRESS, I.E. OUR CHILDREN."
> —CHERYL BRODY (MY SISTER AND MOTHER OF NINE)

ANOTHER WAY TO LOOK AT STRESS: External Stress and Internal Stress

External stressors include:

Physical environment: noise, bright lights, too much heat, confined spaces.

Social (interaction with people): rudeness, bossiness or aggressiveness on the part of someone else.

Organizational: rules, regulations, "red tape," deadlines.

Major life events: death of a relative, lost job, promotion, new baby, divorce or ending a relationship with a significant other.

Daily hassles: commuting, misplacing keys, mechanical breakdowns.

Dating: the hard-to-find soul mate (or two)

Internal stressors include:

Lifestyle choices: poor eating habits, not enough sleep, slouching, overloaded schedule, not exercising, not seeing a chiropractor.

Negative self-talk: pessimistic thinking, self-criticism, over-analyzing.

Mind traps: unrealistic expectations, taking things personally, all-or-nothing thinking, exaggerated or rigid thinking.

Stressful personality traits: Type A, perfectionist, workaholic, or pleaser.

BIO-ELECTROMAGNETIC ENERGY

People give off a subtle energy that affects their environment. If you spend time with stressed-out people their "vibrations" may affect you and cause you to go into a stress response. So choose your friends carefully. If you work with the public, it can be stressful. People may slime you with their unhappiness.

THE STRESS EQUATION

Hans Selye, an early researcher in the science of stress, discovered in the 1950s that different kinds of situations bring on different kinds of stress. The "high" that results from stressful but productive work is beneficial, while stress resulting from illness, embarrassment or failure wears a person down emotionally and physically. Selye believed stress triggers the same biochemical reactions in the body, regardless of whether the situation was positive or negative.

The stress equation has a few more variables. What kind of situation the stress stems from and how a person perceives and copes with stress are both powerful factors. Procrastinators, for instance, usually have all the resources and time they need to finish a task, but they put unnecessary strain on themselves by blowing it off until the last possible minute due to psychological blocks.

When given adequate experience and practice to handle a situation, people experience little stress. But before we get to the tricks and exercises that can help you overcome 'bad' stress, let's break down its psychological and physiological mechanisms.

THE MECHANISMS OF STRESS

> "IF YOUR TEETH ARE CLENCHED AND YOUR FISTS ARE CLENCHED, YOUR LIFESPAN IS PROBABLY CLENCHED." —ADABELLA RADICI

Just like your leg pops out when you tap your knee, stress is an automatic and instinctive response to unexpected events. There are two types of instinctive stress responses that are important to how we understand stress and stress-management.

1. The short-term "fight-or-flight" response is a basic survival instinct.
2. The General Adaptation Syndrome develops after lengthy and sustained exposure to stress.
3. A third mechanism comes from the way you think and how you process your environment. This mechanism is learned, not instinctive.

These three mechanisms can be part of the same stress response, but let's first look at them separately.

16 FIGHT OR FLIGHT

"WHEN EVERYTHING'S COMING YOUR WAY, YOU'RE IN THE WRONG LANE." — ANONYMOUS

Early research on stress, conducted by Walter Cannon in 1932, established the existence of the fight-or-flight response. Cannon's work showed that when an animal experiences a shock or feels threatened, it releases hormones (like adrenaline) that help it survive. And you can go from calm to fight-or-flight mode in seconds.

These same hormones are supposed to help humans escape a dangerous situation or fight for survival. They increase your heart rate and blood pressure, delivering more oxygen and blood sugar to power your most important muscles. They increase sweating in an effort to cool these muscles and help them stay efficient. They redirect blood away from the skin to the core of your body, reducing blood loss if you get hurt. Mentally, the hormones focus your attention exclusively on the threat.

Your pupils dilate to let in more light. Your immune system is depressed (more colds and flu and possibly cancer). Your heart starts pounding faster. Your stomach starts dripping hydrochloric acid. Your blood pressure rises. Your liver produces a lot more cholesterol (heart disease). Your bone marrow produces more platelets making your blood thicker (heart disease). Your breathing is more shallow. Blood is decreased to your intestines and goes to your legs and arms, preparing you to fight or run. Adrenaline and cortisol pump through your body. There's also a decrease in sex hormones. (That's right, no nookie when you're stressed.)

If you don't fight or flight, the cortisol accumulates as a toxin to the body and can make you sick and crazy (and hungry).

IT'S THE CORTISOL, STUPID!

One way you know you're in a fight or flight situation is a voice inside your head that says, "Ya know, I could just slap you in the side of your head." But you don't, and the voice says, "Let's get the hell out of here." And if you don't, cortisol is going to kick your ass. (No, I'm not suggesting that you strangle anyone, just that you rid yourself of cortisol!) Too much cortisol can affect your memory as well.

This adrenaline rush is only helpful if you're fending off an attack from an alligator or running from a herd of blood-thirsty antelope. But in everyday modern life, this instinctual response undercuts your need to be calm, rational, controlled and socially sensitive. You can't work effectively with other people in this pumped-up state because you're excitable, anxious, jumpy and irritable. While these short-lived stress hormones give you a powerful burst of physical strength, they also make your hands shake, undermining precise or controlled movements. The intensity of your focus on survival scrambles your thinking so much it becomes nearly impossible to make a rational decision.

It would be easy to disregard this fight-or-flight response as one triggered only by rare life-threatening circumstances. On the contrary, recent research shows that our bodies go into fight-or-flight mode simply by encountering something unexpected. This hormonal response is actually a normal part of everyday life, although it's often at such a low intensity that we don't notice it.

GENERAL ADAPTATION SYNDROME

Hans Selye took a different approach from Cannon. Starting with the observation that different diseases and injuries to the body seemed to cause the same symptoms in patients, he identified a general response (the "General Adaptation Syndrome") with which the body reacts to a major stimulus. While the Fight-or-Flight response works in the very short term, the General Adaptation Syndrome operates in response to longer-term exposure to stressors.

Selye identified that when pushed to extremes, animals react in three stages:

1. First, in the Alarm Phase, an immediate reaction to the stressor.
2. Next, in the Resistance Phase, the animal adapts to and copes with the threat. This phase lasts as long as the animal can support this heightened resistance.
3. Finally, once resistance is exhausted, the animal enters the Exhaustion Phase and is no longer able to cope effectively.

Selye established this with many hundreds of experiments performed on laboratory rats. However, he also quoted research carried out on bomber pilots during World War II. Once they had completed a few missions over enemy territory, these pilots usually settled down and performed well. After many missions, however, pilot fatigue would set in as they began to show "neurotic manifestations."

In the business environment, this exhaustion is seen in "burnout." The classic example comes from the Wall Street trading floor: by most people's standards, life on a trading floor is stressful. Traders learn to adapt to the daily stressors of making big financial decisions, and winning and losing large sums of money. But in many cases, these stresses increase and fatigue begins to take over.

At the same time, as traders become successful and earn more and more money, their financial motivation to succeed can diminish. Ultimately, many traders experience burnout. We look at this in more detail in our section on burnout.

Much of the stress we experience is subtle and occurs without making an obvious threat to survival. Most comes from things like work overload, conflicting priorities, inconsistent values, over-challenging deadlines, conflict with co-workers, unpleasant environments and so on. Not only do these reduce our performance as we divert mental effort into handling them, they can also cause a great deal of unhappiness.

> "THERE CANNOT BE A STRESSFUL CRISIS NEXT WEEK.
> MY SCHEDULE IS ALREADY FULL." — HENRY KISSINGER

STRESS, A MATTER OF JUDGMENT

In becoming stressed, people must therefore make two main judgments: firstly they must feel threatened by the situation, and secondly they must doubt that their capabilities and resources are sufficient to meet the threat.

How stressed someone feels depends on how much damage they think the situation can do them, and how closely their resources meet the demands of the situation. This sense of threat is rarely physical. It may, for example, involve perceived threats to our social standing, to other people's opinions of us, to our career prospects or to our own deeply held values.

Just as with real threats to our survival, these perceived threats trigger the hormonal fight-or-flight response, with all of its negative consequences.

We've been looking at the Fight-or-Flight response, the General Adaptation Syndrome and our mental responses to stress as separate mechanisms just for clarity's sake. In fact, they can combine together in one response.

> "HALF OUR LIFE IS SPENT TRYING TO FIND SOMETHING
> TO DO WITH THE TIME WE HAVE RUSHED
> THROUGH LIFE TRYING TO SAVE." —WILL ROGERS

THE EMOTIONAL SYMPTOMS OF STRESS

When people are stressed emotionally they default into unhappy emotions like frustration or self-loathing. They often simply feel less capable emotionally of handling stressful situations.

Emotional stress effects include:

Anger and irritability

Feeling critical of self and others

Depression

Feeling overwhelmed

Sense of loneliness

Mood swings

Restlessness

Panic and anxiety

Short temper

> THE COGNITIVE SYMPTOMS OF STRESS "THE HURRIER
> I GO, THE BEHINDER I GET." —UNKNOWN

Yes, stress affects your mind as well. It can prevent you from feeling as if you are thinking clearly.

Intellectual stress effects include:

Forgetfulness

Lack of attention to details

Lack of concentration

Feeling preoccupied

Reduced creativity

Loss of objectivity

Racing thoughts

Indecisiveness

Willing to commit a crime

Considering breaking some or all of the Ten Commandments

Something I've noticed with many people who are going through divorce is that they would repeat themselves daily with no memory of having said the same damn thing yesterday and the day before.

Also I attribute much of the fighting and "criminal acts" during and after divorce to be a form of "temporary insanity" brought on by the stress of divorce.

THE PHYSICAL SYMPTOMS OF STRESS

There is a definite connection between your physical well being and your stress level. In fact, the people who live the longest and are in the best health get stressed the least.

Physical effects from stress include:

Chronic fatigue

Weight gain or weight loss

Headaches

Insomnia

Tight muscles

Stomachaches

Ulcers

Hyperactivity

Constipation

Frequent urination

Loss of sex drive

Cholesterol increase

Heart disease

Hardening of the arteries

High blood pressure

Type II adult onset diabetes

Most forms of strokes

And worst of all: spinal misalignment (when the little bones that make up your back bone come out of whack and irritate nerves)

THE BEHAVIORAL SYMPTOMS OF STRESS

Eating more or occasionally less

Can't sleep or waking often

Isolating yourself from others

Procrastination, neglecting responsibilities

Using alcohol, cigarettes or drugs to suppress or forget emotions

Nervous habits (e.g. nail biting, pacing)

Teeth-grinding or jaw-clenching

Overdoing activities (e.g. exercising, shopping)

Overreacting to unexpected problems

Picking fights with others

Fatigued, tired and run down,

Eating comfort food (ice cream or a box of Oreos)

OTHER EFFECTS OF STRESS

Stress has also been found to damage the immune system, which explains why we catch more colds when we are stressed. It may intensify symptoms in diseases that have an autoimmune component, such as rheumatoid arthritis. Stress also seems to affect headaches and irritable bowel syndrome, and there are now suggestions that stress facilitates cancer by interfering with the immune system.

Stress is also associated with mental health problems and, in particular, anxiety and depression. Here the relationship is fairly clear: the negative thinking that is associated with stress also contributes to these conditions.

However, if you suspect that you are prone to stress-related illness, or if you are in any doubt about the state of your health, you should consult appropriate medical advice immediately. Keep in mind that stress management is only part of any solution to stress-related illness. Or as my friend, Dr. Carl Wolstrom, a family psychiatrist, once said, "Besides talk therapy and lifestyle changes, many patients respond to medicine." He called it "better living through chemistry."

WORK STRESS AND BURNOUT

> "ONE OF THE SYMPTOMS OF AN APPROACHING NERVOUS
> BREAKDOWN IS THE BELIEF THAT ONE'S WORK IS TERRIBLY IMPORTANT."
> — BERTRAND RUSSELL, PHILOSOPHER

Work is usually just that—work—but it's not supposed to be a hazard to your health! Unfortunately for a lot of people, it is. Stress at work causes more health complaints than even financial worries or family problems.

The National Institute for Occupational Safety and Health reports that:

> 40% of workers reported their job was very or extremely stressful.
>
> 25% view their jobs as the number one stressor in their lives.
>
> Three-fourths of employees believe that workers have more on-the-job stress than a generation ago.
>
> 29% of workers felt quite a bit or extremely stressed at work.
>
> 26% of workers said they were "often or very often burned-out or stressed by their work."

In today's economic environment, upheavals, downsizing, layoff, merger and bankruptcies have cost hundreds of thousands of workers their jobs. Millions more have been shifted to unfamiliar tasks within their companies and wonder how much longer they will be employed. Adding to those pressures, workers face new bosses, computer surveillance of production, fewer health and retirement benefits, and the feeling they have to work longer and harder just to maintain their current economic status. Employees at every level are experiencing increased tension and uncertainty and are updating their resumes.

A SENSE OF POWERLESSNESS

A feeling of powerlessness is a universal cause of job stress. When you feel powerless, you're prey to depression's traveling companions, helplessness and hopelessness. Worst of all, you don't alter or avoid the situation because you feel nothing can be done.

Secretaries, teachers, waitresses, middle managers, police officers, court reporters and mail handlers (why do they go "postal"?) and chiropractors (just kidding) are among those with the most highly stressed occupations. The highest number of heart attacks and deaths from heart attacks occur on Monday mornings. People have heart attacks in response to their jobs. Workers have to respond to others' demands and timetables, often with little control over events or outside pressures. These workers complain of too much responsibility and too little authority, unfair labor practices and inadequate job descriptions. Employees can counteract these pressures through workers' unions or other organizations, grievance or personnel offices or, more commonly, by direct negotiations with their immediate supervisors.

WHAT'S SO DIFFERENT ABOUT TODAY'S WORKPLACE?

Studies from organizations such as National Institutes for Occupational Safety and Health and the American Psychological Association show the following changes in working conditions have overburdened our traditional coping mechanisms:

- Growing psychological demands as we increase productivity and work longer hours
- The need to gather and apply growing amounts of information
- Job insecurity
- The need for both men and women to balance obligations between work and family as women enter the workforce worldwide

AMERICANS ARE WORKING LONGER AND HARDER

A 1999 government report found that the number of hours worked increased eight percent in one generation to an average 47 hours per week with 20 percent working an average of 49 hours per week. U.S.

workers put in more hours on the job than the labor force of any other industrial nation. According to an International Labor Organization study, Americans put in the equivalent of an extra 40-hour work week in 2000 compared to ten years previously. Japan had the record until around 1995, but Americans now work almost a month more than the Japanese and three months more than Germans. We are also working harder. In a 2001 survey, nearly 40 percent of workers described their office environment as "most like a real life survivor program.

ABSENTEEISM DUE TO JOB STRESS HAS ESCALATED

> "THERE IS NOTHING SO DEGRADING AS THE CONSTANT ANXIETY ABOUT
> ONE'S MEANS OF LIVELIHOOD...MONEY IS LIKE A SIXTH SENSE WITHOUT
> WHICH YOU CANNOT MAKE A COMPLETE USE OF THE OTHER FIVE."
> — WILLIAM SOMERSET MAUGHAM, BRITISH PLAYWRIGHT AND NOVELIST

According to a survey of 800,000 workers in over 300 companies, the number of employees calling in sick because of stress tripled from 1996 to 2000. An estimated one million workers are absent every day due to stress. In fact, over half of the 550 million working days lost annually in the U.S. from absenteeism are stress-related. One in five of all last-minute no-shows are due to job stress. If key employees are doing this, it can have a domino effect that spreads down the line to disrupt the operation of an entire workplace. Unanticipated absenteeism is estimated to cost American companies $602 per worker every year and the price tag for large employers could approach $3.5 million annually. A 1997 three-year study conducted by one large corporation found that 60 percent of employee absences could be traced to psychological problems caused by job stress.

THE WORKPLACE HAS BECOME DANGEROUS

Some jobs are inherently dangerous and others can suddenly become so. Criminal justice personnel, police officers, firefighters, ambulance drivers, military personnel and disaster teams witness many terrible scenes and are routinely exposed to personal danger. Most of these workers handle such incidents capably. But occasionally a particularly bad episode will stay with them, appearing in memory flashbacks and nightmares. Sleep disturbance, guilt, fearfulness, and physical complaints may follow. Even ordinary jobs can become traumatic: a coworker, boss or client physically threatens an employee; a bus crashes on a field trip; an employee is robbed or taken hostage. Such events can create post-traumatic stress disorder (PTSD) and result in workers' compensation claims if left untreated by a trauma specialist.

WORKPLACE STRESS CONTINUES TO GROW (Why do you think they call it work?)

Experts at the Centers for Disease Control and the National Institute for Occupational Safety and Health have been studying the ways stress affects American workers. They've found:

- Stress is linked to physical and mental health problems, as well as decreased willingness to take on new and creative endeavors.
- Job burnout experienced by 25% to 40% of U.S. workers is blamed on stress.
- More than ever before, employee stress is being recognized as a major drain on corporate productivity and competitiveness.

Depression, only one type of stress reaction, is predicted to be the leading occupational disease of the 21st century, responsible for more days lost than any other single factor.

I know what you're thinking. You're thinking that if you could occasionally strangle a co-worker, you'd feel better. Well, I suppose you would. However, it's rude and illegal. So don't do it. Or if you're going to, don't say I said you should.

I know how you feel. Sometimes I used to get hassled by my ex, or as we would call her, "the plaintiff." Well, I thought about getting violent but I never did. And if I had, I certainly wouldn't admit it in a book. Besides, I have an ironclad alibi. And she had it coming!!!! Oh, where was I? Oh yea, violence never solves anything.

WHAT CAUSES IT? (It's all your fault! Just kidding.)

> "WHEN YOU FIND YOURSELF STRESSED, AS YOURSELF ONE QUESTION: WILL THIS MATTER FIVE YEARS FROM NOW? IF YES, THEN DO SOMETHING ABOUT THE SITUATION. IF NO, THEN LET IT GO." —CATHERINE PULSIFER, AUTHOR

Stress may be fueled by a number of factors, including:

- Bad relations with other work colleagues
- Long and/or irregular hours
- Too little work or too much work
- Repetitive work, boredom and lack of job satisfaction
- Working alone
- Job insecurity
- Job or organizational change
- Low pay
- Jobs with heavy emotional demands
- Poor working environments such as excessive noise, the presence of dangerous materials, over-crowding, poor facilities, or extremities of temperature or humidity
- Increased accessibility—the use of mobile phones, pagers and email often means you're expected to be available more easily and more often.

The work situation can be even worse if there's bullying, conflict, harassment or an employer is indifferent to staff needs. If an organization lacks good leadership, the employees feel it: work arrangements, deadlines and demands can get set without consultation and seem to be inflexible. In this kind of work environment, staff uncertainty creeps in—about direction, purpose and job responsibilities. And that's when the stress sinks in, as employees begin to feel powerless and start to worry about what the future holds.

RETIREMENT IS NOT THE ANSWER

After years and years of work that they don't enjoy, many people think that the solution is to quit, or what we euphemistically call "retire." For most people, not working can lead to a form of stress called boredom and inactivity. Often retirees start to "rust out" physically and mentally, leading to an acceleration of the aging process. They become more susceptible to chronic disease and a decrease in mental acuity. Well, if you're saying—"I'm a 70 year old, what should I do? Work forever?"— I'll tell you what I am recommending in the next chapter.

NEGATIVE THOUGHTS CROWD OUR MINDS

> "IN THIS WORLD WITHOUT QUIET CORNERS, THERE CAN BE NO EASY ESCAPES
> FROM HISTORY, FROM HULLABALOO, FROM TERRIBLE, UNQUIET FUSS."
> —SALMAN RUSHDIE, INDIAN-BRITISH NOVELIST AND ESSAYIST

If you try to memorize a long list of words, you won't be able to remember more than six or eight items unless you use formal memory techniques. Similarly, although we have huge processing power in our brains, we cannot be conscious of more than a few thoughts at any one time.

As we become uncomfortably stressed, distractions, anxieties and negative thinking begin to crowd our minds. Your thoughts may begin to race or rattle meaninglessly around your brain. These jumbled thoughts compete with our ability to do work or even function. Concentration suffers, and focus narrows as our brain becomes overloaded. It's a vicious cycle: the more our performance suffers, the more new distractions, difficulties, anxieties and negative thoughts overwhelm our minds.

Stress reduces people's ability to deal with complicated information, make well-informed decisions and be creative. As a result, distressed people will persist in a course of action even when better alternatives are available.

IT'S NOT ALL BAD NEWS...

In my nearly thirty years of chiropractic practice, I've noticed increasing numbers of people come in with complaints about stress and stress-related conditions. The trend is alarming, which is why I think it's no exaggeration to call stress an epidemic.

But, before you let loose with the "Stress Reduction Kit" on the next page, remember that there are some proven methods for conquering stress that don't involve bruises or cracked heads. Following the advice in this book probably won't always be a cake walk—you're going to have to examine the way you lead your life very carefully and critically but in the end, your efforts will be worth it. It's like learning to ride a bike: you may fall down occasionally in the beginning, but pretty soon you'll have the skills to ride around almost any obstacle. Increasing your body's ability to handle or manage stress is the key to this book.

As you'll see in the following chapters, there are many activities you can do to make yourself more stress resilient. Anyone who has accomplished great things like you have will be under stress. The solution is not merely stress avoidance. The solution is stress resilience, as you will soon see.

STRESS REDUCTION KIT

**BANG
HEAD
HERE**

DIRECTIONS

1. Place kit on FIRM surface..
2. Follow directions in circle of kit.
3. Repeat step 2 as necessary, or until unconscious.
4. If unconscious, cease stress reduction activity.

IMPORTANT TERMS & NOTES

1. Only matured, physically and mentally well-behaved adults with an IQ above 120 are recommended to use this anti-stress kit.
2. It is advisable that the user call and wait until the ambulance has arrived before using this anti-stress kit.
3. User should realize that the insurance will not cover anything destroyed/broken/cracked/injured/etc. due to this anti-stress kit.
4. Use this anti-stress kit at your own risk!

CHAPTER 2

LAUGHING, LOVING, LIVING: WHAT YOU CAN DO TO HANDLE OR MANAGE STRESS SO YOU CAN BE STRESS-FREE AND HAPPY!

> "STRESS...THE CONFUSION CREATED WHEN ONE'S MIND OVERRIDES THE BODY'S BASIC DESIRE TO CHOKE THE LIVING DAYLIGHTS OUT OF SOME JERK THAT DESPERATELY DESERVES IT." —UNKNOWN

When you do certain activities your body makes chemicals that act as an antidote or an "anti-stress" response to strengthen your ability to deal with stress. During these stress-relieving activities, your body produces endorphins and serotonin as well as other hormones like dopamine.

34   Many research papers have been written about the positive effects of serotonin and endorphins on the body. Some of the most common prescriptions in this country are drugs that artificially increase the amount of serotonin in the body so people feel happier.

However, drugs have side effects. So one of the key components of this program is for you to increase your serotonin and endorphin levels naturally by engaging regularly in activities that make you more stress-proof.

What activity you choose depends a lot on your personality and needs. No activity is the magic answer for everyone, because we're all unique. No one on earth has your fingerprints or your exact DNA. Just as no two snowflakes are alike, no two people are the same. So your prescription for the good life will be unique (you little snowflake)!

What do you love to do?

About twenty years ago I took a personal and career development workshop by a man named Martin Sage. He kept asking me what I really wanted to have, to do and to be. Then, he helped me find what activities I could do to make me happier and more productive. When I utilize my natural talents, my eyes get brighter and I become rejuvenated. Going after what you want could help you with your stress.

> "WHEN I AM OVERWHELMED, I TURN TO THE THREE WISE MEN: HAAGEN-DAZS, BEN AND JERRY." — CARLY SMITH

THE JOY SOLUTION: WHAT DO YOU LOVE TO DO?

> "THE GREATEST WEAPON AGAINST STRESS IS OUR ABILITY TO CHOOSE ONE THOUGHT OVER ANOTHER. " —WILLIAM JAMES, AMERICAN PSYCHOLOGIST AND PHILOSOPHER

It's important to your stress level and your happiness quotient that you have at least one activity you do regularly just for the fun of it. Hobbies and other fun activities provide an enjoyable way to sharpen skills, express your creativity or use your natural talents. Also, when you get really engrossed in an activity you enjoy, you experience a state of being known as "flow." When you're in the "flow," your brain is in a near-meditative state, which benefits your body, mind and soul.

Hobbies and enjoyable activities can also be a great way to relieve stress. In fact, many hobbyists have told me that they'd originally started learning about their area of interest as a coping mechanism for stress and that their hobbies continue to be a great source of relaxation and stress-relief.

Remember, this is your only shot at life, so you'd better be enjoying it. Our culture tends to frown on fun and enjoyment, as if it were only a reward for accomplishing some goal. How many times have you heard someone say, "I'll be happy once I lose ten pounds," or "I'll do that once I save up enough money," or "I'll really enjoy my life once my kids grow up and go off to college"?

These sorts of excuses for not being happy or living life fully won't stop until we purposefully and consciously choose to think outside the cultural paradigm. I'm all about having pleasure be at the center of our focus and having enjoyment be at least a daily occurrence.

THE FUN SOLUTION: THE MAGIC OF THE "F" WORD

> "I CANNOT AND SHOULD NOT BE CURED OF MY STRESS,
> BUT MERELY TAUGHT TO ENJOY IT." — HANS SALEY, THE
> "FATHER OF STRESS MANAGEMENT"

One of my favorite words is the "F" word. And the "F" stands for Fun. Life has to be fun. Isn't that what we wish everyone when we send birthday and holiday greetings? Our greetings send a message for a healthy, happy and vibrant life. What if every single day of our life could be like that?

Fun does not mean excessive, irresponsible or silly. It reflects a certain attitude and willingness to do what you want. Having fun means creating more opportunities to dance and feel the joy of living. When we are experiencing fun, we are living in the moment, with a smile on our face and a twinkle in our eye – and we're spreading that attitude to everyone around us. Fun is contagious!

Have you ever thought about how many words have fun as their root—and we miss the point! Take the word Fundamental for example. Fundamental means the basics. The first three letters spell fun. That means enjoyment needs to be the basis for just about everything we do. If you're working at a job and not having fun or enjoying it, it may be high time for some changes.

When you were very young, life was a "barrel of laughs." But when we turned five or six, were told to "behave" so we could go to school and become molded into proper human beings. Life now consisted of "homework," and our internal fire was doused out, the light in our eyes diminished and life maybe wasn't as fun after all.

So, start having fun now, not tomorrow. Why wait? You can still lose those ten pounds, save up that money and HAVE FUN. Like John Lennon said, "Life is what happens to you while you're busy making other plans." If life is going to happen to you anyway, you might as well enjoy it in the meantime!

"TRUE HAPPINESS IS HAVING ONE'S PASSION AS A PROFESSION." — MARTIN SAGE

THE PASSION SOLUTION: WHAT ARE YOU PASSIONATE ABOUT?

"A TRULY HAPPY PERSON IS ONE WHO CAN ENJOY
THE SCENERY ON A DETOUR." — ANONYMOUS

Coming right along on the heels of fun is passion. What brings you the most enjoyment, passion and energy in your life? If you are doing those enjoyable things on a regular basis, you'll feel not only fully alive and energized, but guess what? You won't be feeling stressed and headed towards burnout. One of the secrets I've found after working with people for nearly thirty years as a chiropractor is that people who consistently follow their passion and concentrate on bringing more joy to their lives are much healthier, more fun to be around and more youthful than those who don't enjoy their lives.

Finding your passion isn't always easy. One of the secrets to success is to first discover what activities bring you joy and utilize your natural talents, and then make that joy at least a part of your career. You are a unique individual, endowed with many traits that make you special. Pay attention to your energy when you do certain things, are around certain people or walk into specific situations. Begin noticing the energy level around you. Pay attention to how it changes.

So, here's how to start the process. First, make a list of all your gifts. In other words, what talents or characteristics do you possess that make you stand out? What makes you unique? What comes easily to you? Include on your list even those areas where you are a contrarian or deviant or rebel. These can be powerful and positive qualities, too. Your power lies in this list.

Now make a second list of all those activities you love to do or feel passionately about. Include the answer to this key question: what do I give that fills me with joy when I'm giving it? Chances are, you love giving what you have in abundance. And what do you have in abundance? Those gifts or talents you put on the first list.

It would be helpful to consider WHY you like a certain activity. What are the qualities of a particular activity that feeds your passion? If something lights your fire, then you must have some insight into why and how it does. Write down what it is about it that inspires you, what pleases you, what reveals more of your soul to you, what makes you laugh and what contributes to a greater good.

Now, think of activities that involve several of your talents, gifts, passions and unique characteristics at the same time. We want to kill two (or more) birds with one stone or, better put, hug two or more birds with one embrace.

The more passions and gifts you can make intersect at one point, the better.

If, for some reason, that intersection of passions does not have a commercial component, modify it with more passions or talents until it does. At the intersection of many passions and talents, there should emerge a service, a product, an artwork or a body of information that can be spun off commercially. This way you get to pursue your passions, grow your talents, give of yourself to others, contribute to a greater good and, as a by-product of all this playing around, generate wealth.

Other questions to explore:

> What one subject do you enjoy talking about for many hours?
>
> What do you dream of doing that you've never told anyone about?
>
> Do any of your hobbies involve working a lot with other people?
>
> What specific concerns preoccupy your mind, breaking into whatever else you're thinking about?
>
> What do you do in your daily life that makes you feel most alive?
>
> If you could do anything for the rest of your life and not be concerned about money, what would you do?
>
> What do you most enjoy doing for others?
>
> Let's pretend you've reached the end of your life, and you're looking back on it. What's the one thing or place you want to be most happy about having done or having been?
>
> Who in the world have you come to care about the most? Who do you most want to help, enable or reach? (Define the categories however you want. Go with your first instincts.)

Write down at least five of your life experiences that gave you the strongest sense of fulfillment and/or growth. Don't worry about what others would say about them. In fact, don't analyze them at all until later—just write them down for now. It's just a stream of consciousness exercise. If more experiences come to mind, just keep listing them until you exhaust yourself. You'll sort them out later.

When you've gone through all of these questions, start to look for patterns, underlying themes and common traits to the answers you gave. Who else benefited from your passion, and what was your role in creating that benefit? Did you discover abilities you didn't know you had? What were they? Did any of the answers give you thrills? Tears? Whittle it down, focus on the strongest themes and work toward a list of things that stand out to you.

If you come to a conclusion, then you have discovered a passion that is rooted deep within you and has already had a strong impact on your life. That passion needs direction. And after doing this self-evaluation, you have a good place to start the adventure.

Here are some other ways to connect with your passion:

1. Get Curious—Curiosity is the basis of passion. Shake off everything you think you know and begin from the view that you are almost completely ignorant on the subject. Then look for novelty to boost your interest.

2. Set a Goal—Create a specific goal, along with a deadline. This can infuse mundane activities with a sense of direction and purpose. Reaching that goal might involve working extra hours to save up money or doing research on a subject before you leap into it. If you look at these simply as steps along the way to your goal, it won't seem boring or like drudgery.

3. Express Yourself—Like that En Vogue lyric, "Free your mind and the rest will follow!" If you're expressing yourself freely, even during "routine" activities, hidden opportunities will present themselves. This could mean inventing a style for folding clothes

or finding a beat for a new song as you're stuck in traffic listening to construction work. It could mean changing the format you write code in or finding a way to spice up the style of your work presentations. View each activity as an act of expression and originality. The only truly boring activity is the one you don't pay attention to.

4. Jigsaw Piecing—A jigsaw puzzle has hundreds of uniquely shaped pieces of a picture. View your activities as pieces of a larger image. This can turn dull activities into parts of a more fascinating whole.

5. Connect with Talents—How can you apply your existing talents to an activity? Find ways to use skills you already have in a new endeavor. An artistic person could draw pictures to study chemistry or history more effectively. An athletic person might be able to use that strength and endurance while giving a speech.

6. Leech Enthusiasm—Energy is contagious. If you spend time with someone who exudes passion, some of it will rub off on you. Seek out people who have the energy you want and get them to describe their motivation. Often it will point you to key information you had no idea could be so interesting.

7. Get Instruction—Finding a teacher can give you the basic level of understanding necessary to enjoy an activity. Sometimes passion can dry up because of not knowing the basics.

8. Focus on the Immediate—Look at the next immediate step. Don't concern yourself over what needs to be done next month or next year if it overwhelms you. Focus on each step of the marathon, not how many miles you have left.

9. Play—If the process confuses or bothers you, just play with it. Don't have a purpose until you can define one.

ENTERING A STATE OF "FLOW"

> "I HAVE MORE ZITS NOW THAN I DID AS A TEENAGER.
> STRESS ZITS." — TIFFANI-AMBER THIESSEN, ACTRESS

When you are completely engrossed in what you're doing, you are normally able to concentrate and focus all of your attention on the important task at hand. When you can get into that kind of zone without distraction, you often enter what Professor Mihaly Csikszentmihalyi from the University of Chicago describes as a state of "flow." This involves "being completely involved in an activity for its own sake. The ego falls away. Time flies. Every action, movement and thought follows inevitably from the previous one, like playing jazz. Your whole being is involved, and you're using your skills to the utmost."

You perform at your best in this state of flow because you are so focused. All of your efforts, resources and abilities are going into what you're doing. When you get motivated like this, you're able to resist competing temptations and won't get so stressed that anxieties and distractions interfere with clear thought.

This is an intensely creative, efficient and satisfying state of mind. It is in this state of mind, for example, that the most profound speeches are made, the best software is developed and the most impressive athletic or artistic performances are delivered.

SIMPLE WAYS TO ENJOY YOUR DAILY LIFE MORE

> "THERE ARE THOUSANDS OF CAUSES FOR STRESS, AND ONE ANTIDOTE TO
> STRESS IS SELF-EXPRESSION. THAT'S WHAT HAPPENS TO ME EVERY DAY.
> MY THOUGHTS GET OFF MY CHEST, DOWN MY SLEEVES AND ONTO MY PAD."
> — GARSON KANIN, AMERICAN WRITER, ACTOR AND FILM DIRECTOR

Any activity you enjoy acts as a buffer against stress. Hobbies keep you from focusing too much on the burdens of your daily life, but they also boost your ability to deal with those same burdens more easily and efficiently.

Learn

Studying subjects that interest you can be a stress-buster. I listen to books on tape and CD's of lectures, sometimes an hour or two a day. Plus, when I'm listening to the wise and profound words of my favorite authors, like Martin Sage or Brian Tracy, that nagging little voice inside my head has to shut up.

Some religious people study the Bible for hours on end. If you're into it, that could be your stress-buster. Here are some other resources to check out:

Universities and community colleges
Foreign language classes
Cooking classes
Dance lessons
Exercise classes
Writing workshops
Playing a musical instrument

Explore photography

Whether you want to learn to take better pictures of your friends and family or delve into the world of creating fine art, photography can be a great hobby. As you practice seeing the world through the eye of a photographer, you may begin to notice more in the world around you.

The end result: not only do you have a diverting hobby and an activity to call your own, but also you'll be looking for beauty or fascinating scenes everywhere you go!

Paint, draw or create any form of art

Painting and other art projects carry the same stress management benefits as photography. You can get in touch with your artistic side and use drawing as a way to process emotions, distract yourself and relax. As an added benefit, art pieces make great gifts and are a wonderful way to share yourself with others.

Reading

Remember to read for pleasure—whatever you want, whatever interests you, not what you think you SHOULD be reading. Look at it as a relaxing escape or means of self-improvement. When you feel like your life is getting chaotic and unmanageable, head to a bookstore or a library for some peaceful reflection.

> "THE TIME TO RELAX IS WHEN YOU DON'T HAVE TIME FOR IT."
> —SYDNEY J. HARRIS, JOURNALIST

Spend time in Nature

One way to increase physical activity and de-stress is to spend time outdoors. It's often more fun to be physically active while outdoors. Plus, exercising outdoors increases aerobic benefits. Getting your blood pumping and the sweat running—or just taking in some deep breaths of crisp air outside in the cooler months – will clear your mind and can help get your thoughts back on a positive track.

There are a number of simple ways you can participate in outdoor activities alone or with friends:

- Have a picnic. You can eat your evening meal in your back yard or pack a lunch to take to your neighborhood park.
- Go on a walk. Look for interesting shapes and colors in nature while you are on your walk. Listen to the birds. Take a close look at the ground, the trees and the sky. You'll soon start to notice all the things you've been missing by being too wrapped up in your mind with worries.
- Take your work outside. Find a quiet area free from distractions and work outdoors.
- Listen for sounds in nature as you sit outside with friends or family. Discuss what your heard. Did you hear the same things? Different things? Anything new?
- Take a walk just after it has rained. What do you see as signs of the rain? How does it feel outside? What do you smell?
- Visit a lake, river or creek. Are there different smells here? Are different plants and animals living here?
- Set up an obstacle course using items such as chairs, boxes, sticks and balls. Make up the rules and play an impromptu game.
- Remember: from earth we came and to earth we will return. Anything we do in nature can be nurturing. Take gardening, for example. Did you know that locally grown fruits and vegetables, like from your backyard, can be healthier for you than those produced hundreds or even thousands of miles away?
- Spending time outdoors has a positive impact on our well-being. Fresh air cleans out the lungs, helps reduce stress, provides us with a natural learning environment and gives us something fun to do with other people.

I encourage you to go outside, even for just five minutes. The naturalist John Muir said, "In every walk with nature, one receives far more than he seeks."

I go for walks through the woods on a regular basis, weather permitting. And no, I don't hug trees. Well, there was that one time, but no one was around. And don't kiss a tree like Molly Shannon did in that movie Superstar!

Sunlight

Many of us need natural sunlight on a regular basis to feel good. Perhaps ten minutes a day. Seasonal Affective Disorder (SAD) is a form of temporary mild depression caused by a lack of sunlight in the winter. For us North Americans, artificial full spectrum light may help, but I personally prefer a few days in the tropics come January.

Start an aquarium

Watching aquarium fish swim around has proven health benefits, including reduced blood pressure and stress relief. Maintaining an aquarium of beautiful fish requires regular (but not overwhelming) attention, has the potential to connect you with other saltwater fish enthusiasts and provides you with the opportunity to create something unique: your own mix of fish, rocks, and plant life.

Fish murdering

Oh yeah, you call it fishing. Well if you enjoy it, go right ahead—it can be very relaxing for you freaks (just kidding).

Piece together a puzzle

Engaging your mind in a puzzle takes your focus off of what's stressing you and develops your brainpower at the same time. As a bonus, you get a nice break, experience some "flow," and come back to your problems with a fresher, stronger mind, which can help you handle life's stressors better.

Ride a bike

When we rush around in our cars all day we often miss interesting scenes on city streets or the natural beauty of the country. When you're on a bicycle (or if your like me, a pair of rollerblades), life passes at a slower, more manageable pace. But be careful out there: make sure you have the proper equipment for high visibility, especially if you're riding on busy roads. Because if you break your neck, that's a bad thing.

Garden

Like bicycling, gardening gets you out into the sunshine and fresh air. While you're at it, you're creating more beautiful surroundings to come home to each day.

Listen to music

They call it the "Mozart Effect." Studies show that if you listen to classical music, you can go into a meditative state of relaxation. I think any music you enjoy can increase your endorphins and serotonin. On the other hand, some health clubs I go to play this loud, crappy music that makes me want to throw a dumbbell at someone's head. But to each his or her own, I suppose.

48 Play the piano or any other musical instrument

Listening to music can be its own hobby, but creating music is an even more powerful stress-relieving way to pass the time. It absorbs your attention fully and becomes a vehicle for creative expression. Getting together with other people to play music is a great way to share your talents and forget your worries.

Singing

Many people have a singer inside them and when they sing, endorphins and serotonin skyrocket. Try karaoke and see how you feel afterwards. Don't get drunk the first time, it may backfire. Having an audience of admirers for any performance can be quite nurturing and helps boost self-esteem. And that's partly why I teach, perform, give presentations and speeches: group admiration.

Write

Whether you're writing in a personal journal, as an amateur author or even as a professional, putting your thoughts down on paper is cathartic and relaxing, and provides something great to share with others. Many people find that journaling has a calming effect because it helps them sort out problems. When you're stressed out and your thoughts are racing or jumbled, tell yourself, "I'll write it down and then I won't think about it!" More often than not, you'll get so wrapped up in writing down your thoughts that you'll "flow" right into relaxation.

Get a pet (or an animal companion)

Pets provide unconditional love and support. They help people combat loneliness and offer a wonderful sense of support. They also provide physical contact for people. A study in London's Hyde Park showed that pet owners, when they were with their dogs, talked to more people and had more extensive conversations than when they were alone. A Swedish study found that 57 percent of pet owners said their dogs had helped them make friends.

Pets force their owners to take walks and care for someone else, all activities that enhance self-esteem and get your mind off stress!

A University of Maryland study suggested that pets can help bring families closer together by reducing conflict and tension and increasing play among family members. Remember how important play is? Pets love to play.

If you have a dog and a significant other and they made a law in your town that you can only have one or the other, who goes? The dog or the spouse? People love their doggies.

THE PEOPLE SOLUTION: THE IMPORTANCE OF SOCIAL SUPPORT

> "MEN FOR THE SAKE OF GETTING A LIVING FORGET TO LIVE." —MARGARET FULLER, JOURNALIST

WHAT THE DOCTORS SAY

According to a 1999 Harvard study, people who have an active social life live nearly two and a half years longer than reclusive people. This means it's important for you to go out with friends, have dinner parties, play cards with friends, play around, and just generally be around people. Another study from Carnegie Mellon University showed that people with regular social contact had a 20 percent greater immune function than those who don't.

The lesson: BE SOCIAL!

There is a form of torture called solitary confinement. You may have seen Tom Hanks in the movie where he was dying of loneliness, (thank God for Wilson, the ball!). Studies on social support show that having one or two close and supportive friends is at least as valuable to emotional health as having a large group of friendly acquaintances or more shallow friendships. However, having social support from several supportive friends would be the best of both worlds.

There are some good reasons to have at least a few different friends to fall back on: If you have only one person supporting you through a difficult time, you may wear that person out or feel unsupported if that person is unavailable. It's better for everyone if you have at least a few people you can depend on. Relationships change as you age, but it's never too late to build friendships or choose to become involved. The investment in social support will pay off in better health and a brighter outlook for years to come.

It's important to note that social support isn't the same as attending a support group. Social support is a network of family, friends, colleagues and other acquaintances you can turn to, whether in times of crisis or simply for fun and entertainment. Support groups, on the other hand, are generally more structured around meetings or self-help sessions, often run by mental health professionals.

Simply talking with a friend over a cup of coffee, visiting with a relative or attending a church outing is good for your overall health. If you have a mental illness, these connections can help you weather troubled times. Your friends and social contacts may encourage you to change unhealthy lifestyle habits, such as excessive drinking or being inactive. Or they may urge you to visit your doctor when you feel depressed, which can prevent problems from escalating.

Social support can also increase your sense of belonging, purpose and self-worth, promoting positive mental health. It can help you get through a divorce, a job loss, and the death of a loved one or the addition of a child to your family. And you don't necessarily have to actually lean on family and friends for support to reap the benefits of those connections. Just knowing that they're there for you can help you avoid unhealthy reactions to stressful situations.

How to Meet New People:

Some people benefit from large and diverse social support systems, while others prefer a smaller circle of friends and acquaintances. In either case, it helps to have plenty of friends to turn to. That way, someone is always available when you need him or her, without putting undue demands on any one person. You don't want to wear out your friends.

If you're not still in school or you're not working for a large company with a built-in social structure and constant opportunities to meet new people, it's still easy to build new friendships. Here are a few ways to meet people:

- Join a gym—If you're not comfortable striking up a conversation with the person on the next Stairmaster, most gyms offer yoga, aerobics or even martial arts classes, which provide a intimate setting with more opportunities to strike up a conversation or find a workout buddy.
- Get involved in a hobby—If you enjoy making things with your hands, perhaps you can enroll in a community art class. If you like writing, a writer's workshop will provide a great opportunity to improve your writing skills and get to know other writers at the same time. Joining a class geared toward your interest guarantees that you'll improve your skills and meet people with whom you already have something in common.

Do lunch—Invite an acquaintance to join you for breakfast, lunch or dinner.

Volunteer—Getting involved with a charity you believe in will give you a sense of doing something positive to help the world. Not only will you be relieving stress by lending a hand and getting your mind off your own problems, you'll meet people with similarly big hearts and a great passion for helping.

Get a pet—You can derive physical and emotional benefits from being a pet owner, as already mentioned, but you can also meet other pet owners at dog parks or pet stores. There are even park days for passionate rabbit owners! Let your 'best friend' help you connect with other (human) friends.

Throw a party—If you invite all of your current friends and encourage each to bring a friend, you'll have a pool of new people to meet. Plus, you may inspire your friends to host their own parties, where you'll meet even more new people.

Smile!—This one may sound simple, but if you give off an approachable vibe, you may find that you're striking up conversations with new people wherever you go. Not all these conversations need to lead to a new friendship, but some might, and just one warm exchange with someone new can brighten up your day (and theirs).

THE TAKE-TIME-OFF SOLUTION: GO ON A VACATION

"BABIES DON'T NEED A VACATION, BUT I STILL SEE THEM AT THE BEACH… AND IT PISSES ME OFF! I'LL GO OVER TO A LITTLE BABY AND SAY, 'WHAT ARE YOU DOING HERE? YOU HAVEN'T WORKED A DAY IN YOUR LIFE!'" —STEVEN WRIGHT, COMEDIAN

If you haven't taken a vacation yet this year, or at least some time off from your job, do it. Yes, as a chiropractic physician, I am prescribing you a vacation, and the sooner the better!

Jobs can be greedy, gobbling up all the time we give them. In a country where we have six weeks less time off per year than our Western European counterparts, nearly half of U.S. employees feel overworked, according to the Families and Work Institute. That overwork has serious implications for safety in the workplace, job performance, job retention and health care costs. Yet, a full 25 percent of U.S. employees don't even take the vacation they're entitled to because of job demands.

Vacations are an important rest, recovery and renewal strategy for creating work/life balance—especially in our fast-paced, 24/7 world. They provide an opportunity to recharge our batteries so that we can return to work refreshed.

"Taking a vacation is not a luxury—it's a necessity," said Kathleen Hall, founder of The Stress Institute in Atlanta, in an interview with MSNBC. "If you don't have the opportunity to relax and reflect you get stressed, and chronic stress is the driver of most diseases—heart disease, obesity, insomnia."

Think of your vacation not as a break but as a boost that may make you even better at your job. "People have false beliefs about productivity," Hall added. "They think it means going full force without breaks. But what we know from research in organizational psychology is that taking time off can enhance productivity."

Going on vacations prolongs your life. Researchers from the State University of New York at Oswego conducted a survey of more than 12,000 men ages 35 to 57 who had participated in a large heart disease prevention trial. The results, presented March, 2007 at a meeting of the

American Psychosomatic Society in Savannah, GA, suggest that men who take vacations every year reduce their overall risk of death by about 20 percent, and their risk of death from heart disease by as much as 30 percent. To their surprise, the researchers discovered that some of the men surveyed didn't take any vacation time over the five years surveyed. But instead of being rewarded for dedication to their jobs, they suffered the highest overall death rate and highest incidence of heart disease of any of the participants. And once they were dead, they couldn't work anymore.

"We concluded that skipping vacations could actually be dangerous to your health," Brooks Gump, Ph.D., one of the study's co-authors, told Vegetarian Times. "Vacations have a protective effect because they help you reduce your load of stress, or at least allow you to take a break from the everyday stressors of the workplace."

Like with all advice, you should test it and see how it works for you. Personally, I'm not a fan of vacations and I rarely take them. I prefer to go to seminars on personal development, which I find rejuvenating (if the location is exotic, so much the better).

> "THE MARK OF A SUCCESSFUL MAN IS ONE THAT HAS SPENT AN
> ENTIRE DAY ON THE BANK OF A RIVER WITHOUT FEELING GUILTY ABOUT IT."
> —ANCIENT CHINESE SAYING

EXAMPLES OF MINI-VACATIONS

You don't always have to take a week in Hawaii to feel the benefits of being on a vacation. Here are some simple ideas for short vacations you can take on a weekly or even daily basis:

Day spas
Romantic getaways
Movie dates

Camping trips

Sporting events

Visiting a museum or art gallery

Taking the day off and staying in bed

Concerts

Going on a drive for the afternoon

Beaches

Botanical gardens

Biking trips

Naps

Smoke pot (just kidding, I wanted to see if you were paying attention)

THE LAUGHTER SOLUTION: LAUGHTER THERAPY

"THE HUMAN RACE HAS ONLY ONE REALLY EFFECTIVE WEAPON, AND THAT'S LAUGHTER. THE MOMENT IT ARISES, ALL OUR HARNESSES YIELD, ALL OUR IRRITATIONS AND RESENTMENTS SLIP AWAY, AND A SUNNY SPIRIT TAKES THEIR PLACE." — MARK TWAIN

Research has shown that laughter has both preventative and therapeutic values. When you laugh, you're inhaling deeper than normal and sending ample supplies of oxygen into your blood, the lifeline of our system. On average, children laugh 400 times per day, and adults only laugh 15 times per day. So if laughter is so good, why aren't we doing more of it? Maybe gyms and health clubs should add a 'laughing room' right next to the weights room and sauna.

Laughter helps alleviate the negative effects of stress, which can rightly be called the number one killer today if you consider at all the diseases linked to it: high blood pressure, heart disease, anxiety, depression, frequent coughs and colds, peptic ulcers, insomnia, allergies, asthma, menstrual difficulties, tension headaches, stomach upsets and even cancer. Laughter helps boost the immune system, which is the master key to maintaining good health.

Other benefits of laughter:

- Helps control high blood pressure and heart disease. While there are many factors for these like heredity, obesity, smoking and excessive intake of saturated fats, stress is one of the major factors. Laughter keeps blood pressure low by reducing the release of stress-related hormones and relaxing the body.
- Increases stamina through increased oxygen supply.
- Alleviates pain and creates a sense of well being from released endorphins, the body's painkiller hormones.
- Effective antidote for depression, anxiety and psychosomatic disorders: laughter boosts the production of serotonin, a natural anti-depressant.
- Gives an excellent internal massage to the digestive tract and enhances blood supply to important internal organs like the liver, spleen, pancreas, kidneys and adrenal glands.
- Laughter ensures good sleep and reduces snoring because it exercises the muscles of the soft palate and throat.
- Brings a happy glow to your face and makes your eyes shine with a thin film of tears which are squeezed from the lachrymal sacs when you laugh.

Laughing is a powerful form of exercise that gives you more of a cardiovascular workout than many "regular" aerobic activities.

In a nation that spends billions of dollars every year on prescription drugs, not to mention illegal drugs, we sometimes overlook the coping mechanisms nature endowed us with. Our bodies were created to take care of themselves for the most part, and we sometimes botch things up when we try to alter our system with drugs. Studies have proven that when we laugh, there is an actual chemical change in our bodies that helps to ease pain and release stress. Laughter is a coping mechanism for the normal stresses of life. Laughter also releases endorphins in the brain; endorphins are neurotransmitters that attach to the same receptors in our brains as the opiates. Opiate drugs make us lose touch with reality and numb pain. Since laughing releases the endorphins in our brain, it's like taking opium or morphine without the adverse side effects.

What is laughter? Laughter is a form of 'eustress' (the opposite of distress) and it releases those feelings of anxiety that wreck chemical havoc on the body. Laughter is like doing sit-ups; that's why your stomach sometimes feels sore after a good belly laugh. Just as with exercise, there are two stages to laughter: the arousal phase, when the heart rate increases, and the resolution phase, when the heart rests. Laughing gives the diaphragm, abdominal, intercostals, respiratory accessory and facial muscles a complete workout. Some people, depending on how they laugh, may even use their arm, leg and back muscles when laughing. Nearly 2000 years ago, the physician Galen noticed that cheerful women were less likely to get cancer than depressed women. John Steinbeck once said, "A sad soul can kill you quicker, far quicker, than a germ."

Turns out, modern science proves them both right. Laughter's ability to fight malignant cell growth has added exciting new possibilities in cancer research. Some of the studies performed by O. Carl Simonton, M.D. and Stephanie Matthews-Simonton lead us to believe that a person's emotional status may affect their likelihood of getting or overcoming cancer. Perhaps if people would start relieving their stress through laughter before they get cancer, we would see a reduction in the number of cancer patients altogether!

Norman Cousins, the man who started the laughter health craze, was editor of the Saturday Review for over thirty years and has written numerous books, including Anatomy of an Illness. In August 1964, Cousins came home from a meeting in Moscow with a fever, feeling achy all over. Within a week he could not move. He was eventually diagnosed with a collagen illness that attacks the connective tissues of the body. He started reading material about stress and how it can wear down your immune system. He came across a book by Hans Selye called The Stress of Life, which proposed that negative emotions cause stressful and harmful effects on the body. He hypothesized that if bad emotions are harmful, then good emotions should be healthful.

At the time, the hospital was mostly trying to keep Cousins out of pain since there was no cure or treatment for his disease. He was being given the maximum amount of drugs every day. Realizing that that much of the medicine was very toxic, he decided to try laughter as a cure. He moved home and hired a nurse to oversee his medical treatment. His nurse would also show him Marx Brothers films and read humorous stories and books to him. Within days he was off all painkillers and sleeping pills and had discovered that ten minutes of genuine belly laughter gave him two hours of pain-free sleep.

Do we laugh because we are happy, or are we happy because we laugh? Both of these are probably true, but we usually only exercise the former. Laughter is a fascinating phenomenon that works like medicine. Think of this: although most drugs affect everyone differently, laughter affects everyone the same way. It exercises your entire body and makes you feel relaxed and pain free.

> SO WHY NOT LAUGH? MAYBE WE'LL START SAYING, "A LAUGH
> A DAY KEEPS THE MEDICAL DOCTOR AWAY." "FOR FAST-ACTING RELIEF,
> TRY SLOWING DOWN." —LILY TOMLIN, COMEDIAN

HOW TO USE LAUGHTER

You can raise your laughter level with the following:

- T.V. and movies - There's no shortage of comedies out there, both at the theater and in the aisles of video stores, as well as right on your TV. Don't waste your time watching something marginally funny; find shows or movies that are truly hilarious and watch them frequently.

- Laugh with friends - Going to a movie or comedy club with friends is a great way to get more laughter in your life. The contagious effects of laughter may mean you'll laugh more than you otherwise would if you were alone, plus you'll have jokes to reference later. Having friends over for a party or game night is also a great setup for laughter and other good feelings.

- Find humor in your life - Instead of complaining about life's frustrations, try to laugh about them. If something is so frustrating or depressing that it verges on the ridiculous, realize that you could look back on it and laugh. Think of how it will sound as a story you could tell your friends, and then see if you can laugh about it now. With this attitude, you may also find yourself being more lighthearted and silly, giving yourself and those around you more to laugh about. If you approach life in a more mirthful way, you'll stress less and laugh more, guaranteed.

Fake it until you make it - Just as studies show the positive effects of smiling occur whether the smile is fake or real, faked laughter also provides the benefits of real laughter. So smile more and fake laughter; you'll still achieve positive effects, and that fake merriment may soon lead to real smiles and laughter.

THE SEX SOLUTION

If you're a child of mine, don't read this next section.

Speaking of sex, recently I went to the doctor and he asked if I had had sex this week, and I said, "No, my birthday isn't until August."

Sex is more important to some people than others. I think it's more important for male people, but I suppose it depends on the person. It works better if you're in love with your sex partner and vice versa. And it's less effective if you're having sex by yourself.

While most of us generally recognize that extremely uptight and stressed-out people could benefit from a nice roll in the hay, sex isn't always included as a top stress management technique. With all the physical and emotional benefits it provides, it should be! A healthy sex life has stress management benefits and can even help you get your groove back if stress has put a damper on your libido.

In addition to effectively taking your mind off your worries for a decent period of time, sex provides some of these other stress busters:

> Deep Breathing: This deep, relaxed type of breathing relaxes your body, oxygenates your blood and reduces the stress you feel.
>
> Sense of Touch: Studies show that massage can be a great stress reliever.

Endorphins and Serotonin: Sexual activity releases endorphins and other feel-good hormones.

Physical Workout: Depending on your level of enthusiasm, you can burn a lot of calories during sex and gain the stress management benefits of exercise, too.

SOMETHING THAT FEELS GOOD IS GOOD FOR US!

Many of us were told growing up that sex was something we should stay away from, or at least not talk about. But sensuality is an innate part of our being. Luckily, it's never too late to reap the health benefits of sex. Whether you're a young man or a granny, it's time to stop thinking of sex as just another "guilty pleasure" and celebrate in the knowledge that it's good for your health. Here's why:

Sex helps ease pain. Have you ever noticed that while you are intimate with a partner, it's much easier to forget about the aches and pains in your body? Women in two small studies have noticed that their tolerance for pain increases while they are sexually stimulated. This may be because stimulation and orgasm lead to the release of corticosteroids and endorphins that increase our pain thresholds, providing short-term relief for women with menstrual cramps, migraines, back pain or arthritis.

Sex improves mood and decreases depression. The same endorphins that ease our pain can make us feel euphoric after having sex. And this doesn't change, as we get older.

Sex can boost your ego. I think most men consider sex the "ultimate compliment." Conversely, when someone is turned down for sex, or in other words when she says "No," it's the "ultimate insult."

Sex relaxes your tensions. Some people describe reaching orgasm as the ultimate release. It is the moment when they can let everything go. That's no surprise, because oxytocin, the hormone that both sexes release during sex, relaxes and calms people. Of course you should only have sex with someone you're married to (yeah right!). And don't call me to write a prescription for sex. Besides, where would you get it filled? A bar perhaps.

REDUCING STRESS AT WORK

> "PRESSURE AND STRESS IS THE COMMON COLD OF THE PSYCHE."
> — ANDREW DENTON, AUSTRALIAN COMEDIAN

Work can be a stressful place, wherever you earn your living, whether in an office, a factory or a school. Some stress is good: deadlines and competition can motivate us and push us to create a better product, a more streamlined plan or a more creative approach.

But when work expectations push stress levels over the limit, those same motivators make us irrational and can, quite literally, kill us. Fortunately, there are specific steps you can take that will help you reduce your stress at work and better cope with it.

1. Improve your time management and organization skills
   Plan ahead. Sit down and make a list what you need to do. Avoid vague or intimidating tasks like, "Improve networking skills" or "Write 100-page research proposal." Break it down; think day-by-day. Otherwise, you're just setting yourself up for more stress. Decide when your work needs to be done and plan accordingly. If you have an excessive workload, try delegating some of it. Just because you could do all the work doesn't always mean you should: there's no shame in getting help on a project or giving someone else a few tasks. Also, learn to say "no" to extra work

projects. Be careful not to set unrealistic goals. You need to be honest with yourself about your own abilities and limitations.

2. Relax and breathe deeply
   I'll be getting into more in depth relaxation techniques in the next chapter, but it's well worth repeating a couple tips here. Whether you are overwhelmed by the amount of work in front of you or involved in a dispute with a co-worker, take a few deep breaths through your nose. You can't get as worked up or anxious if you force yourself to breathe through your nose. Try taking a deep breath through your nose right now: you'll probably sit up straighter and feel your shoulders relax.

3. Take more breaks from your work
   Even a five-minute break will help. Get away from your desk. Go for a walk—outside is better, but simply climbing up two flights of stairs and back down is good, too. A Harvard Medical School study found that as little as 10 to 15 minutes a day of private time can increase productivity and cut down on stress, headaches, colds and poor sleep.

4. Lighten up
   Smile more. Crack a joke with your co-workers. You will be amazed at how much more pleasant the people around you are when you make an effort to be pleasant yourself.

5. Learn to listen better
   Rather than getting upset when others disagree with you, listen actively and find the areas of agreement. Be assertive and stand up for yourself, but don't be rigid.

6. Fix your environment
   Make whatever adjustments you need to in the lighting, temperature, noise level and other controllable factors in your office.

7. Don't sweat the small stuff
   Realize that there are some things that just aren't worth worrying about, and there are some things you just can't change. Don't waste time stressing over either.

8. Find a mentor or a friend
   Having someone to talk with at work makes it easier to joke around, get advice and create collaborative solutions. I've always have several mentors or coaches to help me with my life and career.

9. Spend more time with optimistic people
   Avoid negative or gossipy co-workers. They will only pull you down to their level and add to your stress. Choose to work with people who have a positive attitude instead.

10. Eat lunch away from your work
    If you're in the midst of a project, it's probably a temptation for you to eat a sandwich in front of your computer while reading emails or getting other work done. Or maybe you skip lunch altogether to get a leg up on your ever-lengthening to-do list. These are both bad choices and will ultimately cause more stress (even if you initially feel you're avoiding stress by getting more done). Lunch is a great opportunity to get out for a break, eat with co-workers or meet a friend. Skipping lunch altogether depletes your energy. Don't be tricked by the surge of adrenaline energy you get from working on an important project; sooner or later, you'll feel drained and your productivity will take a nosedive.

11. Attend a career or personal development seminar
    My most effective stress-busting technique has always been in the form of workshops or seminars in conjunction with coaching. Every few months for nearly thirty years, I have attended weekend seminars on career or personal development. My favorite by far is the Martin Sage program (see the References section). I have also attended over one hundred chiropractic workshops and

have found them to be quite inspiring and motivating. So attend programs in your chosen field. Plan to be the best at what you do. Remember, do what you love as much as possible.

OH, #@%& STRESS!

According to a BBC News report from 2007, swearing at work can help employees deal with stress. A study by Norwich University found that the use of "taboo language" increased team spirit. Obviously, it's not good to swear around customers or clients, but employees who "swear together" boost solidarity and cope with stress better.

THE POWER OF POSITIVE THINKING

> "MOST FOLKS ARE ABOUT AS HAPPY AS THEY MAKE UP THEIR MINDS TO BE." —ABRAHAM LINCOLN

"Think positive!" You probably hear this advice a lot when you're worried and feeling down. But most of us never really take this advice seriously. When you're anxious and your thoughts are racing or your head is filled with self-doubt, it can be very hard to imagine that you can actually control your thoughts. But you DO have control. You have the power to trick your mind into thinking happier and calmer thoughts.

Just like fake smiles can lead to real smiles, faking a good attitude even when you're feeling down in the dumps can lead to an authentic positive outlook on life.

Positive thinking is a mental attitude that unlocks your mind's potential for thoughts, words and images that are conductive to growth, expansion and success. A positive mind anticipates happiness, joy, health and a successful outcome of every situation and action. It's important to remember this: whatever the mind expects, it finds. So, let it find some good vibes!

When our attitudes are positive, we entertain pleasant images and constructive ideas. We see in our mind's eye what we really want to happen. This brings brightness to our eyes, boosts our energy and eventually gives us real, honest-to-goodness happiness. Instead of getting caught in a vicious cycle of negative thinking, you can bring about a cycle of happiness – one that feeds itself on good thoughts and will bring you success.

Positive thinking affects more than just your mind. Your physical being will be changed for the better. When you're allowing yourself to think positively, you walk tall and your voice gets stronger and more confident. People are drawn like magnets to that kind of body language because it shows that you're a happy, content person.

Positive and negative thinking are both contagious. All of us affect, in one way or another, the people we meet. This happens instinctively and on a subconscious level, through thoughts and feelings transferred through body language. People sense our bio-electro magnetic energy and are affected by how we are feeling. Is it any wonder that we want to be around positive people and shun the negative ones? People are more disposed to help us if we are positive. Whether they are aware of it or not, people dislike and avoid anyone who broadcasts negativity.

Some people are much more sensitive to people's energy and are more aware of their energy. The kind of people who are more aware of and affected by people's energy are people called women.

So you are thinking, does this mean men are stupid? No. Our skin is thicker, our muscles are thicker and our skulls are thicker. We just don't feel the vibrations as much. So men may get stressed out a little less as a result. And if you're a man, that's how she knows you're lying. And she'll hold it against you for a millennium.

You're probably thinking that faking positive thoughts is for other people, those chipper people who never seem to have a bad day, and not for you. But guess what? All truly happy people aren't born that way. Sometimes they have to work at it. Sometimes they feel awful. The difference is that they take the effort to switch around those negative thoughts into positive ones, even if they don't really feel like it at first.

Like all seemingly insurmountable challenges, taking positive thinking step-by-step and day-by-day will make it easier. In order to turn the mind toward the positive, inner work and training are required. Attitude and thoughts do not change overnight.

Persuade yourself to give positive thinking a shot:

> Always visualize the favorable and beneficial options in every situation: the glass really is half-full.
>
> Use positive words in your inner dialogues or when talking with others.
>
> Smile a little more.
>
> Disregard any feelings of laziness or a desire to quit.

Even if the idea seems strange, give it a try. You have nothing to lose, only gain.

THE THINKING SOLUTION: CHANGE YOUR PERCEPTIONS OF STRESS

> "SUCCESS IN LIFE IS DETERMINED 10% BY WHAT HAPPENS TO YOU AND 90% BY HOW YOU REACT TO IT." —LOU HOLTZ, FOOTBALL COACH

Quite often, our experience of stress comes from our perception of the situation. Often that perception is right, but sometimes it's not. Often we are unreasonably harsh with ourselves or instinctively jump to the wrong conclusions about other people's motives. This can send us into a downward spiral of negative thinking that can be hard to break.

When people feel stressed, they have made two main judgments. First, they feel threatened by the situation, and second, they believe that their capabilities and resources are not enough to meet the threat. How stressed someone feels depends on how much damage they think the situation can do to them, and how closely their resources meet the demands of the situation.

Situations are not necessarily stressful in their own right. Rather it is our interpretation of the situation that drives the level of stress we feel.

Quite obviously, we are sometimes right in how we perceive something. Some situations may actually be dangerous, may threaten us physically, socially or in our career. In these situations, stress and emotion are an important part of the early warning system that alerts us to the threat.

Very often, however, we are overly critical and unjust with ourselves in a way that we would never be with friends or co-workers. This, along with other negative thinking, can cause intense stress and unhappiness that severely undermines self-confidence.

You are thinking negatively when you fear the future, put yourself down, criticize yourself for errors, doubt your abilities or expect failure. Negative thinking damages confidence, harms performance and paralyzes mental skills.

Unfortunately, negative thoughts tend to flit into our consciousness, do their damage and flit back out again, without us noticing their significance. Since we barely realize they were there, we do not challenge them properly.

> BECOME AWARE OF YOUR AUTOMATIC THOUGHTS! "YOU DON'T GET ULCERS FROM WHAT YOU EAT. YOU GET THEM FROM WHAT'S EATING YOU." —VICKI BAUM, AUSTRIAN AUTHOR

I had a terrible time with stage fright for many years. I would always think that Murphy's Law would hold true while I was giving a speech. My self-talk was very negative but after a lot of speeches the nervousness started to decrease.

One approach to combat this nervous stress is to observe your "stream of consciousness" as you think about the situation or topic that's stressing you. Do not suppress any thoughts. Instead, just watch them run their course and write them all down. Then let them go. Picture them just floating away.

Here are some typical negative thoughts you might experience when preparing to give a major presentation:

- Fear about the quality of your performance or of unexpected problems that may interfere with it.
- Worry about how the press or audience (especially important people in it like your boss) may react to you.
- Dwelling on the negative consequences of a poor performance.
- Self-criticism over a less-than-perfect rehearsal.

Since you can't manage thoughts you're not aware of, thought awareness is the first step in the process of managing negative thoughts.

KEEPING A STRESS JOURNAL

A stress journal can help you identify the regular stressors in your life and the ways you deal with them. Each time you feel stressed out, keep track of it in your journal.

Write down:

> What caused your stress (make a guess if you're unsure).
>
> How you felt, both physically and emotionally.
>
> How you acted in response.
>
> What you did to cope or feel better.

Putting your worries on paper has a marvelous way of clarifying things. As you keep a daily log, you will begin to see patterns and common themes. Your journal may help you see that you don't really have that much to worry about, or it may bring overlooked problems to light. Whatever your discoveries, your stress journal should help you establish a plan for moving forward.

RATIONAL THINKING

> "STRESS IS LIKE AN ICEBERG. WE CAN SEE ONE-EIGHTH OF IT ABOVE, BUT WHAT ABOUT WHAT'S BELOW?" —ANONYMOUS

The next step in dealing with negative thinking is to challenge the negative thoughts that you identified using the stress journal. Look at every thought you wrote down and challenge it rationally. Ask yourself whether the thought is reasonable. What evidence is there for and against the thought? Would your colleagues and mentors agree or disagree with it?

The following challenges could be made to the negative thoughts identified earlier in the speech scenario:

* Feelings of inadequacy: Have you trained yourself as well as you reasonably should have? Do you have the experience and resources you need to make the presentation? Have you planned, prepared and rehearsed enough? If you have done all of these, you've done as much as you can to give a good performance.

* Worries about performance during rehearsal: If some of your practice was less than perfect, then remind yourself that the purpose of the practice is to identify areas for improvement and problems so that these can be sorted out before the performance.

* Problems with issues outside your control: Have you identified the risks of these things happening and have you taken steps to reduce the likelihood of them happening or their impact if they do? What will you do if they occur? And what do you need others to do for you?

* Worry about other people's reactions: If you have put in good preparation and you do the best you can, then you should be satisfied. If you perform as well as you reasonably can, then fair people are likely to respond well. If people are not fair, ignore their comments and rise above them.

Tip:

Make sure you take the long view about incidents that you're finding stressful. Put it in perspective. Just because you're finding that new system or those new responsibilities stressful now doesn't mean that they will ALWAYS be so for you in the future.

When you challenge negative thoughts rationally, you should be able to see quickly whether the thoughts are wrong or whether they have some substance to them. Where there is some substance, take appropriate action. However, make sure that your negative thoughts are genuinely important to achieving your goals, and don't just reflect a lack of experience, which everyone has to go through at some point.

AVOID UNNECESSARY STRESS

Not all stress can be avoided, and it's not healthy to avoid all potentially stressful situations. You may be surprised, however, by the number of stressors in your life that you can eliminate by using these basic rules-of-thumb:

- Learn how to say "no" – Know your limits and stick to them. Whether in your personal or professional life, refuse to accept added responsibilities when you're close to your limit. Taking on more than you can handle is a surefire recipe for burnout.

- Avoid people who stress you out – If someone consistently causes stress in your life and you can't turn the relationship around, limit the amount of time you spend with that person or end the relationship entirely.

- Take control of your environment – If the evening news makes you anxious, turn the TV off. If traffic's got you tense, take a longer but less-traveled route. If going to the market is an unpleasant chore, do your grocery shopping online.

- Avoid hot-button topics – If you get upset over religion or politics, cross them off your conversation list. If you repeatedly argue about the same subject with the same people, stop bringing it up or excuse yourself when it's the topic of discussion.
- Pare down your to-do list – Analyze your schedule, responsibilities and daily tasks. If you've got too much on your plate, distinguish between the "shoulds" and the "musts." Drop tasks that aren't truly necessary to the bottom of the list or eliminate them entirely. There is no need to overwhelm yourself.

In the next chapter, we'll be covering ways to reduce your physical reactions to stress with relaxation techniques.

MURPHY'S LAW ON LIFE

1. An easily–understood, workable falsehood is more useful than a complex incomprehensible truth.
2. By working eight hours a day, you may actually get to be boss and work 12 hours a day.
3. Never try to teach a pig to sing. It wastes your time and annoys the pig.
4. You get more with a kind word and a gun that you can with a kind word.
5. Opportunity knocks at the least opportune time.
6. The bigger they are, the harder they hit.
7. If one views his problems closely enough he will recognize himself as part of the problem.
8. The only imperfect thing in nature is the human race.
9. Leftover nuts never match leftover bolts.

10. People are always available for work in the past tense.

11. If a man says to you, "It's not the money, it's the principle," I bet you six to one it's the money.

12. Love is blind, but lust doesn't give a good G-D Damn.

13. Almost anything in life is easier to get into than out of.

14. When anything is used to its full potential, it will break.

15. The best way to make fire with two sticks is to make sure one of them is a match.

16. Measure twice because you can only cut once.

17. All the cookies are not in the jar.

18. Never step in anything soft.

CHAPTER 3

THE RELAXATION SOLUTION: MEDITATION, SPIRITUALITY, DEEP BREATHING, CALMING YOUR MIND AND CHILLIN'

"TENSION IS WHO YOU THINK YOU SHOULD BE. RELAXATION IS WHO YOU ARE."
—CHINESE PROVERB

Stress builds up tension in your body. You know how tension feels: your muscles are tight, your mind races, your body gets surges of adrenaline and cortisol. Tension happens all over your body, from neck pain to stomach cramps, from a racing heart rate to hunched-up shoulders.

RELAXATION is an important part of taking good care of yourself. It's a common enough word, yet very few of us have had much experience with real relaxation. By "real relaxation" we don't mean mindless exercise, zoning out, socializing or pursuing some distraction like television, a computer game or a book. Of course, all those activities can be great antidotes to stress, but only if you're also learning and practicing relaxation techniques. Deep relaxation is a focused, intentional period of time when we're mindful and alert, yet our muscles are relaxed. Sound easy? Well, it's not always as easy as it sounds. But once you get good at it, relaxation can restore energy, improve mood and boost performance levels better than practically any other activity.

Relaxation should be a core technique on your quest to beat stress. It's a full mind-and-body process that decreases the wear and tear of life's challenges on you. Practicing relaxation techniques can improve how you physically respond to stress by:

Slowing your heart rate

Lowering blood pressure

Slowing your breathing

Reducing the need for oxygen

Increasing blood flow to major muscles

Reducing muscle tension

You may also gain overall health and lifestyle benefits from relaxation techniques:

Fewer physical symptoms, such as headaches and back pain

Fewer emotional responses, such as anger and frustration

More energy

Improved concentration

Greater ability to handle problems and conflicts

More efficiency in daily activities

Practicing systematic relaxation is an important part of allowing the mind and body to be still and access the peace within you. As you learn how to mindfully relax, you'll become more aware of muscle tension and the other physical manifestations of stress. Once you know exactly how your stress responses feel, you can make a conscious effort to practice a relaxation technique the moment they start to take over your body. This can prevent stress from spiraling out of control.

Relaxation techniques take practice. Remember that this kind of relaxing is a learned skill. And as with any skill, your ability to relax improves with practice. Be patient with yourself. Give yourself time. Stay motivated to reduce the negative impact of stress on your body and to experience a greater sense of calm in your life.

This chapter will explore various ways you can achieve real relaxation. The techniques range from meditation to visualization exercises to improving sleep, but they all have a common goal: helping you bring calm into your life so you can better cope with stress.

I. MUSCLE RELAXATION EXERCISES

Both of these exercises are best done lying on the floor, with palms facing up, although they can also be done sitting or standing. I recommend sticking with each exercise for ten minutes. Less than seven minutes is not enough to feel the full effects of the relaxation, and more than 15-20 minutes is too long and can cause sluggishness or sleep. If you're not noticeably more relaxed by the finish, you might increase the time, and if you get spacey or feel shaky, you should shorten the length of the exercise.

Maintain an even flow of deep breathing throughout the following exercises. If you worry about staying with the exercise too long or not long enough, set a stopwatch the first few times so you know what ten minutes or fifteen minutes feels like.

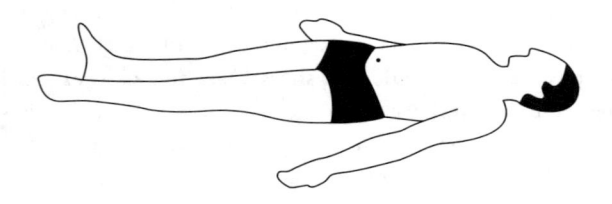

Tension/Relaxation Technique

Lie quietly on the floor with a small pillow under your neck and arms by your side, palms facing upward. Feel your body become heavy and allow yourself to rest into the pose.

Then, tighten and hold all the muscles of your face—forehead, eyes, nose, mouth, cheeks, ears. Scrunch up every muscle in your face, hold and then release it. Let go of the tension you were carrying and become aware of the relaxation spreading across your face.

Going through the body systematically, tense and release each of the major muscle groups. Tense your shoulders by lifting them up toward your ears, hold for a few seconds and then release.

Make your hands into fists and tighten all the muscles of your arms and then release.

Take in a deep lungful of air, expanding the chest and upper back. Exhale. Relax the chest and upper back.

Tense your abdomen, feeling it harden like a rock, and then release. Let your abdominal muscles soften.

Squeeze the buttocks together and hold, feeling the tension. Then release the buttocks and allow them to relax into the floor beneath you.

Point your toes and tense both legs. Really squeeze with all the energy you've got! Then, release the tension and let your legs to fall into the floor.

Now, tense the whole body at once. Squeeze the muscles of the face, shoulders, arms and hands, chest and upper back, abdomen, buttocks and legs, and point your toes. Put every ounce of energy you've got into tightening every muscle. Hold the tension and then release it, allowing the whole body to melt.

Let a deep feeling of relaxation spread throughout your entire body. Let the floor support you as you sink into it, feeling waves of peace and relaxation. Feel the breath coming in nourish you and the breath going out cleanse you.

Rest quietly for five to ten minutes, remaining alert and mindful of each breath.

When you are ready, roll onto your side and pause for a moment or two before slowly transitioning back up to sitting or standing.

PROGRESSIVE MUSCLE RELAXATION TECHNIQUE

Allow your body to rest on the floor, letting it come to a place of stillness. Establish deep, diaphragmatic breathing, letting your breath become even and undisturbed.

Starting with the top of your head, allow your awareness to travel from your head down to your toes and then from the toes back up to the head, making a mindful progression throughout the entire body.

Become aware of the crown of your head. Allow your awareness to travel to your forehead and temples, resting your eyebrow, eyelids and eyeballs, feeling them sink back into their sockets.

Bring your attention to the tip of your nose, feeling the coolness of the breath coming in and the warmth of the breath going out. Rest here for a several breaths.

Let your awareness travel through your face to your cheeks, jaws, mouth, chin and down through your throat.

Allow your neck and shoulders to relax, feeling all the tension from them release as they sink into the floor.

Feel your awareness travel down through your arms—upper arms, lower arms, wrists, hands and fingertips. Rest here for a few moments, feeling the breath travel back and forth from your nostrils to your fingertips.

Let your awareness travel back up through your arms to your shoulders, and then down to your chest, rib cage and around the back to your spine.

Bringing attention to your heart, allowing your awareness to rest here for several breaths. Inhale from the nostrils down to the heart's center and exhale back up to the nostrils. Do this for several breaths.

Allow your awareness to travel down to your abdomen, feeling it rise on the inhale and fall on the exhale.

Let your awareness travel down through your lower back to your groin, hips and buttocks, and then farther down through your upper legs, lower legs, feet and toes. Here again, breathe back and forth from your nostril to your toes for several breaths.

Now, travel back up the body in reverse order, from the toes all the way to the crown of the head. Don't rush through it – take your time.

Stay here in this relaxed state for about ten more breaths, feeling the effects of the relaxation practice on your body, breath and mind.

When ready, turn on to your side, pause for a moment or two, and then slowly come up to sitting or standing.

II. ERASING STRESS AND TENSION

> "IF YOU ASK WHAT IS THE SINGLE MOST IMPORTANT KEY TO LONGEVITY, I WOULD HAVE TO SAY IT IS AVOIDING WORRY, STRESS AND TENSION. AND IF YOU DIDN'T ASK ME, I'D STILL HAVE TO SAY IT." — GEORGE F. BURNS, ACTOR AND COMEDIAN

Often the situations and beliefs that make us feel anxious seem insurmountable. We tend to actually empower stress with mental representations of our situation. In these representations, we look tiny and helpless, while the stressors look huge and unsolvable. But you do have the power to change these mental representations and cut those stressors down to size! The next two exercises will help you gain mastery over stress by learning to shrink it or even erase it with your mind. They will help you put stress in a much more manageable and realistic perspective.

Shrinking Stress

Sit or lie in a comfortable position. Breathe slowly and deeply.

Visualize a situation, person or even a belief that makes you feel anxious and tense (such as, "I'm afraid of the dark" or "I don't want to give that public speech").

As you do this, you might see a person's face, a place you're afraid to go, or simply a dark cloud. Where do you see this stressful picture? Is it above you, to one side or in front of you? How does it look? Is it big or little, dark or light? Does it have certain colors?

Now slowly begin to shrink the stressful picture. Continue to see the stressful picture shrinking until it is so small that it can literally be held in the palm of your hand. Hold your hand out in front of you, and place the picture in the palm of your hand.

If the stressor has a characteristic sound (like a voice or traffic noise), hear it getting tiny and soft. As it continues to shrink, its voice or sounds become almost inaudible.

Now the stressful picture is so small it can fit on the tip of your second finger. Watch it shrink from there until it finally turns into a little dot and disappears.

Often this exercise causes some amusement as the feared stressor shrinks, gets less intimidating and finally disappears. Go ahead and laugh at it. Seeing how ridiculous and funny the stressor looks can relax you even more and help spin a healthier perspective on your life.

Erasing Stress

Sit or lie in a comfortable position. Breathe slowly and deeply.

Visualize a situation, a person or even a belief that causes you to feel anxious and fearful (such as, "I'm afraid to go to the shopping mall" or "I'm scared to mix with people at parties").

As you do this you might see a specific person, an actual place or simply shapes and colors. Where do you see this stressful picture? Is it below you, to the side, in front of you? How does it look? Is it big or little, dark or light, or does it have a specific color?

Now imagine that a large eraser, like the kind used to erase chalk marks, has just floated into your hand. Actually feel and see the eraser in your hand. Take the eraser and begin to rub it over the area where the stressful picture is located. Watch the eraser rub out the stressful picture. See it fade, blur and finally disappear. When you can't see the stressful picture anymore, continue to focus on your deep breathing for another minute, inhaling and exhaling slowly and deeply.

III. BREATH AWARENESS

Quality of breathing is closely related to the nervous system. Short, shallow breathing indicates a disturbed mental state, whereas smooth, deep and even breathing reflects of a calm and balanced state. Over time, either type of breathing can create a permanent state of mind: agitated and stressed, or happy and content. This is why learning to work with our breath is so important—it's the key to our emotional life!

The first step to being able to control your breathing in any situation is to become aware of it. Breath awareness is an essential element of being able to relax and focus the mind and body. The following are a few exercises to help you become aware of your breathing. To do these, find a time and a space for yourself where you will not be interrupted. Remove your shoes and loosen any clothing around your neck, chest, and abdomen.

Spending at least ten minutes on each exercise will help you reap the full benefits.

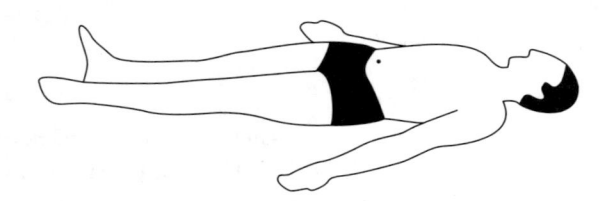

Breath Awareness #1: Corpse Pose (Lovely name, isn't it?)

Lie quietly on the floor with a small pillow under your neck and arms by your side, palms facing upward and toes turned slightly outward. Close your eyes, allowing yourself to rest in this position, what yogis call savasana, or corpse pose.

Relax your abdomen, your back and the sides of your rib cage. Feel your body become heavy. Feel the entire weight of your body just sink into the floor. Let the floor support you. Begin to experience the stillness that is naturally rising up within you. Settle into this stillness and let it support you.

Begin to notice the breath coming in and the breath coming out. Feel the coolness of the breath coming in and the warmth of the breath going out. The breath coming in is nourishing and rejuvenating, and the breath going out is cleansing, releasing you of whatever feelings and sensations you don't want or need. For a few moments, just notice the rise and fall of your chest, as if you are watching waves in the ocean.

Relax the muscles of the rib cage and the sides of the body. Place a hand on your abdomen. Soften it, releasing any tension there, and allow it to rise and fall with each breath. As you inhale, your abdomen should fill with air and rise, and as you exhale, it should deplete of air and fall. If, as you breathe in, your abdomen falls, and as you breathe out, your abdomen rises, you are breathing paradoxically, or chest breathing. Avoid this kind of shallow breathing and try to breathe instead into your belly.

Place your other hand on your chest to see if it is moving. In deep diaphragmatic breathing, the chest barely moves. On the inhale, the diaphragm contracts, pulls the lungs down and fills them with air, causing the abdomen to rise. On the exhale, the diaphragm relaxes, and the lungs deflate, causing the abdomen to fall.

After a few moments, bring your hands back to your sides with the palms facing up and continue to notice your breathing.

Now, relax your efforts to be mindful of your breathing. Just allow the breathing to be effortless, happening of its own accord. You don't have to do anything to control it. Just let it be. The breath will come without jerk, without pause; just smooth, even and effortless. It flows.

After some time, roll onto your side and pause for a moment or two before slowly transitioning back up to sitting or standing.

Breath Awareness #2: Crocodile Pose (Hey, not my name!)

Lie on your stomach and fold your arms with each hand on the opposite elbow. Draw the forearms in slightly so your chest is off the floor and rest your forehead on your crossed arms. Your legs can be slightly apart, toes turned slightly outward. You can also place a blanket or a cushion beneath your upper chest and throat for support.

Close your eyes and relax the face, shoulders, abdomen and legs.

Notice your inhalations and exhalations, feeling the abdomen press against the floor and the lower back and sides of the rib cage expand

and rise on the inhale, and feel the abdomen, low back and sides of the rib cage relax on the exhale.

After some time, you may want to bring your attention to your navel. See if you can soften the muscles there even more. This further calms the nervous system and reduces emotional tension.

Eventually, the breath will become effortless, smooth and deep. Because the arms are raised above the shoulders, the upper chest remains still while the diaphragm becomes more active. That's why this pose is ideal for establishing deep, diaphragmatic breathing. The rise and fall of the abdomen is very pronounced and it takes very little time to achieve a state of deep relaxation in this position.

Rest in crocodile for about five minutes, feeling the effects of the posture.

When you feel refreshed, open your eyes and slowly rise to your hands and knees and then up to sitting or standing

Diaphragmatic Breathing

The diaphragm is the most efficient muscle in breathing. It is a large, dome-shaped muscle located at the base of the lungs. Your abdominal muscles help move the diaphragm and give you more power to empty your lungs.

Diaphragmatic breathing is intended to help you use the diaphragm correctly while breathing to:

    Strengthen the diaphragm

    Decrease the work of breathing by slowing your breathing rate

    Decrease oxygen demand

    Use less effort and energy to breathe

Diaphragmatic breathing technique

Lie on your back on a flat surface or in bed, with your knees bent and your head supported. You can use a pillow under your knees to support your legs. Place one hand on your upper chest and the other just below your rib cage. This will allow you to feel your diaphragm move as you breathe.

Breathe in slowly through your nose so that your stomach moves out against your hand. The hand on your chest should remain as still as possible.

Tighten your stomach muscles, letting them fall inward as you exhale through pursed lips. The hand on your upper chest must remain as still as possible.

You can also practice diaphragmatic breathing while sitting in a chair. Just make sure you're comfortably situated, with your shoulders, head and neck relaxed. Legs should be relaxed and not crossed.

At first, you'll probably get tired while doing this exercise. But keep at it, because with continued practice, diaphragmatic breathing becomes easier. Pretty soon you'll be able to do it without thinking. Practice this exercise at first for about five to ten minutes several times per day. Gradually increase the amount of time you spend on the exercise, and perhaps even increase the effort of the exercise by placing a heavy book on your abdomen.

IV. QUIETING THE MIND AND BODY: MEDITATION

> "THE MAN WHO DOESN'T RELAX AND HOOT A FEW HOOTS VOLUNTARILY NOW AND THEN IS IN GREAT DANGER OF HOOTING HOOTS AND STANDING ON HIS HEAD FOR THE EDIFICATION OF THE PATHOLOGIST AND TRAINED NURSE A LITTLE LATER ON." —ELBERT HUBBARD, WRITER AND PHILOSOPHER

Throughout the day your mind may be inundated with thoughts and fantasies that trigger unhappy feelings. Many of these thoughts replay unresolved issues of health, finances, or personal and work relationships. This relentless mental barrage of unresolved feelings reinforces anxiety symptoms and exhausts you. It's important to know how to shut off the constant inner dialogue and quiet the mind.

I recommend that you use meditation, in its most basic and simple form, to quiet that negative chatter in your head. Whether you are new to meditation or a seasoned veteran, this simplified technique can be very powerful.

Let's face it: most of us are so wrapped up in the outside world that we neglect what is within us. We are out of sync with ourselves – giving too much to the external self while shunning the internal aspects of our being. Meditation helps you ignore the external and direct your attention to the internal.

Meditation also allows you to create a state of deep relaxation, which is very healing to the entire body. Metabolism slows, as do physiological functions such as heart rate and blood pressure. Muscle tension decreases. Brain wave patterns shift from the fast beta waves that occur during a normal active day to the slower alpha waves, which appear just before falling asleep or in times of deep relaxation. If you practice these exercises regularly, they can help relieve anxiety by resting your mind and turning off upsetting thoughts.

These instructions are for a simple, seated meditation that can help you develop inner balance. Before you begin, make the decision to sit down and devote the energy of your mind, body and heart to resting within stillness. This is a time to surrender to wakefulness, mindfulness and awareness. Find a place where you will not be disturbed—a room where no one will come in, where the phone does not ring, where little or no noise can get in, etc.

SOME TIPS TO HELP YOUR MEDITATION:

> "I'VE GOT TO KEEP BREATHING. IT'LL BE MY WORST
> BUSINESS MISTAKE IF I DON'T." — STEVE MARTIN

Controlling Your Breath

At no time during the practice of this technique should you make any effort to control the breath. Let it flow naturally. Gradually, you may notice that the pauses between the inhalation and exhalation are becoming longer. Enjoy these pauses, for they are a glimpse of the deep peaceful state of advanced meditation. As you grow very calm you may notice that the breath is becoming so shallow (or the pauses so prolonged) that it hardly seems necessary to breathe at all.

How Long to Practice

The amount of time you practice is entirely up to you but be sure to end your practice by taking in a deep breath and exhaling three times. Then, keeping your mind focused and your energy completely internalized, try to feel peace, love and joy within yourself. Sit for at least five minutes enjoying the deeply relaxed state you are in.

Where to Meditate

If possible, set aside an area that is used only for meditation. This will create a meditative mood every time you walk in. A small room or closet is ideal as long as it can be well ventilated. Your area can be kept very simple—all you really need is a chair or small cushion to sit on.

Posture for Meditation

There are many ways of sitting that are equally good. You can sit either in a straight-backed chair or on the floor in any of several poses. Two things, however, are essential: Your spine must be straight, and you must be able to relax completely.

Eye Position

Focus your attention at the point between the eyebrows. This area, called "the spiritual eye," is a center of great spiritual energy. Your eyes should be closed and held steady, turned slightly upwards as if looking at a point about an arm's length away and level with the top of your head.

MEDITATION #1: FINDING STILLNESS

It is very important that you are physically comfortable when practicing this meditation. This will help prevent you from becoming distracted by bodily sensations that arise from physical discomfort. It is best if you sit upright in a comfortable chair. Make sure you are free from any tightness or restriction due to clothing.

Take a minute to relax and find peace in your body. Close your eyes and mouth, breathing normally through your nose. If it helps you to release tension, take a few deep breaths.

Your goal is to turn your attention inward, away from the outside world of thought and time, towards the world of emptiness and stillness. Focus solely on your breathing so that you can slowly withdraw from the external, chaotic side of reality. Become aware of your breathing with each inhale and exhale. Once you are aware of your breathing, slowly begin to breathe into your abdomen. In other words, breathe using your diaphragm, not your lungs. The lungs expand downward instead of out during the inhale. If you do not know how to breathe with your diaphragm or it's uncomfortable, then breathe as you normally do.

Keep your attention on your breathing. Feel the inhale and exhale of your breath. Withdraw your attention from thoughts about the past or thoughts about the future. Withdraw your attention from all thoughts and let your attention become more and more immersed in the sensations of your breathing. Using your willpower, hold your attention and just be with your breath.

Continuously recall your mindfulness to the inhale and exhale of your breath. If you find yourself distracted with thoughts, gently bring your attention back to the feeling of your breathing. With each breath, allow yourself to be in the present. When you think about it, only the present actually exists. All else is in your thoughts and memories, which you are setting aside for now.

Now that you're at rest with your breathing, slowly turn your attention inwards and find the stillness in your mind. As you find the silence, stay with it. Become the stillness. There is no reason to have any thoughts right now. You'll have plenty of time during the rest of the day to be with your thoughts. Now is the time for stillness. Feel the silence and rest in it. If you find yourself distracted with thoughts, direct your attention on your breathing again and withdraw from your thoughts. Then slowly turn back towards the silence.

If it becomes difficult to find silence or rest with it, try repeating the word "Om" (as in "dome") in slow repetition. Say the word silently within your mind. Feel the vibration of the word as you repeat it and immerse yourself in it. If you find yourself distracted with thoughts, slowly bring your attention back to the repetition of the word.

Don't worry if you find yourself thinking a lot. That's normal. Over time, you will gain the ability to quiet yourself more and more. Like anything else, it just takes practice.

If you experience some physical discomfort during the meditation, make whatever adjustments you need to bring yourself back into the comfort zone. The adjustments might be very subtle muscular, skeletal or attitudinal shifts. Just do your best to relax and remain as still as possible during your meditation.

Try practicing this meditation once a day in the evening for about 15 to 20 minutes. Make it a special part of your daily routine. As you become accustomed to your practice, add a morning meditation for the same amount of time.

Finding the stillness within will be the most challenging task you can ever face, for silence is totally foreign to the condition of our minds. Learning to find inner stillness is similar to learning a new language. It will take persistent practice on your part. Nevertheless, it's within your reach as long as you stay determined.

You'll feel the effects of mediation in your daily life. Combined with regular exercise, it becomes an excellent stress-reducer. It gives you the opportunity to enjoy a newfound appreciation for life. Meditation is one of life's paradoxes, for within silence is everything.

Meditation #2: Focusing

Select a small personal object that you like a great deal. It might be a jeweled pin or a simple flower from your garden.

Focus all your attention on this object as you inhale and exhale slowly and deeply for one to two minutes.

While you are doing this exercise, try not to let any other thoughts or feelings enter your mind. If they do, just return your attention to the object.

At the end of this exercise you will probably feel more peaceful and calmer. Any tension or nervousness that you were feeling upon starting the exercise should be diminished.

Meditation #3: Keeping It Simple

Sit or lie in a comfortable position.

Close your eyes and breathe deeply. Let your breathing be slow and relaxed.

Focus all your attention on your breathing. Notice your chest and abdomen moving in and out.

Block out all other thoughts, feelings and sensations. If you feel your mind wandering, bring it back to your breathing.

As you inhale, say the word "peace" to yourself, and as you exhale, say the word "calm." Draw out the pronunciation of the word so that it lasts for the entire breath. Breathe in, "p-e-e-a-a-a-c-c-c-e-e-e." Breathe out, "c-a-a-a-l-l-l-l-m-m-m." Or, if you're Jewish, say "SHA" as you inhale and, "LOM" as you exhale. If you're Christian, you can say, "JE" as you inhale and "SUS" as you exhale. Repeating these words as you breathe will help you concentrate and keep your mind from cluttering with thoughts.

Continue this exercise until you feel very relaxed.

V. THE HEALING POWER OF VISUALIZATION AND SELF-HYPNOSIS

> "TO GET TO THE ROOT OF STRESS, WE MUST CHANGE THE
> WAY WE LOOK AT IT FIRST." — ANONYMOUS

A picture is worth a thousand words, so the saying goes. Visualization technique is one way to make those thousand words speak to you and help you heal your stress symptoms.

Visualization, a form of self-hypnosis, helps you create positive mental pictures that are self-suggestive and can change emotions that subsequently have a physical effect on the body.

Each one of us has a belief system that is based on the accumulation of verbal and non-verbal suggestions gathered throughout life. Through patterns of repetition (and their associated rewards and punishment), we learn to create our own perception of reality. In essence, we become what we think.

In healing, repetitive use of positive visualization gives us a new a new way to access the mind-body connection. This connection lets the mind and body work together to foster the healing process of the body on a physical level.

So, how exactly does this work? When we experience an emotion, it generates a feeling that turns into a physical sensation. For example: You are watching a horror movie, you feel frightened and then get a chill up your spine. When you sensed a negative image (danger), it produced an emotion of fear which turned into the physical sensation of chills running up your spine. Visualization technique flips this scenario: it uses positive images to produce positive emotions that manifest into positive physical sensations in the body.

Our thoughts really do directly affect our physical being, specifically the endocrine system. For example, fear is related to the hormone adrenaline. If no fear exists, there is no adrenaline. The same applies in reverse: no adrenaline, no fear. They work in tandem. Whenever an emotion crops up in your brain, a chemical reaction courses through your body.

Here's a little more scientific background before we get to the ins-and-outs of the visualization technique:

The hypothalamus, the emotional center of the brain, transforms emotions into physical responses. It also controls the body's appetite, blood sugar levels, body temperature, adrenal and pituitary glands, heart, lung, digestive and circulatory systems. The hypothalamus is the receptor for neuropeptides, chemical messenger hormones that carry emotions back and forth between the mind and body. Neuropeptides link perception in the brain to the body via organs, hormones and cellular activity. They influence every major section of the immune system to help the mind and body work together as one unit.

The brain is a highly efficient system that is connected to every cell in your body by billions of connections. It is divided into two sides: the left, logical side (words, logic, rational thought) and the right, creative side (imagination and intuition). Day to day circumstances are usually met in a logical, left brain mode; but by yielding to the right, creative side, we actually restore balance to the brain. This balancing act gives us a key to the mind-body connection. The right side of the brain automatically steers you to your goal. It totally accepts what you want to accomplish without giving an opinion and acts upon it without judgment. That's why visualization targets the right, creative side of the brain and not the left, logical side.

Positive thought is essential to producing positive results. Negative thoughts and emotions lower the immune system, while positive thought and emotions actually boost the immune system.

Visualization puts your intention to work—the more specific the intention, the more specific the results. Remember, whatever you believe is what your body will do. So when you are thinking of your intention make sure it is clear, specific and achievable.

VISUALIZATION FOR HEALING

Once you are relaxed, the next step is to actualize your visualization. Think of or speak your intention out loud.

Close your eyes and imagine yourself in the healing process or as you want to be.

Watch as your body heals you.

Feel the healing taking place.

Know the healing is being accomplished.

If you run into difficulties, you may want to try one or more of these methods:

- Use creative imagery like seeing the cells in your body healing you, your immune system fighting off invaders, your pain being taken away by healing mud, or whatever image works for you.
- Imagine yourself in a very beautiful place: whole, healthy and happy.
- Try reading scripts from a visualization or self-hypnosis book.
- Try making your own recorded tape of these scripts. Or, if it makes you self-conscious to hear your own voice, have a friend with a calming voice record the script.

Given time and commitment, visualization can work to boost a stressed body back to health. It's also a powerful reminder that your mind and body, combined, have the strength to help you heal.

Self-Hypnosis

Conducting hypnosis on yourself is another way to h
body work together to beat stress.

Here's a self-hypnosis technique adapted from Betty Erickson, wife of the late American psychiatrist, Dr. Milton H. Erickson. I've found it very useful and easy to do. It's unique because it offers a pre-hypnotic suggestion. In other words, you tell yourself what you want to accomplish before you go into the self-induced trance.

Get comfortable — Look ahead, breathe slowly and relax.

State your goal - Tell yourself why you want to go into self-hypnosis. Say, "I am going into a trance for the purpose of _____. During this self-hypnosis session my unconscious mind will make the adjustments so that _____ occurs naturally and easily."

Say how you want to feel afterward - Tell yourself, "In twenty minutes, I'm going to feel _____."

Induce yourself into the hypnotic state - Notice three things (one at a time) that you see. Go slowly; look at each one for a moment. Now pay attention to the sounds surrounding you and notice, one by one, three things that you hear. Next, become aware of your feelings; notice three sensations, isolating them one by one. Go slowly from one to the next. You can use sensations that normally are outside of your awareness, such as the temperature of your ankle, the feeling of the bottom of your feet, the weight of some piece of clothing, etc. Continue the process using two things you see, then two sounds and then two feelings. Next narrow your focus down to one visual, one auditory and one kinesthetic.

During the trance - Picture something. You can make an image up or just let one happen. Pause and imagine hearing a corresponding sound.

imagine a feeling that goes along with the sound and image. Repeat the process with two images, then two sounds, then two feelings. Repeat using three images, sounds and feelings. If you don't get all the way through, relax. In fact, it's a sign that you've gone deep enough if you lose track of where you are in the process. Just let your mind wander where it will and trust that your unconscious is carrying out the suggestions you gave it. Allow yourself to come out of the trance whenever it feels appropriate. You'll often find that you come out very near the time you suggested at the beginning.

VI. POSITIVE AFFIRMATIONS

> "LIFE IS NOT ORDERLY. NO MATTER HOW WE TRY TO MAKE LIFE SO, RIGHT IN THE MIDDLE OF IT WE DIE, LOSE A LEG, FALL IN LOVE, DROP A JAR OF APPLESAUCE."
> —NATALIE GOLDBERG, AUTHOR AND CREATIVE WRITING TEACHER

Positive affirmations are a great tool to reprogram your unconscious mind from negative thinking to positive thinking. The idea is to take positive statements of what you would like to see manifested, and repeat them enough so that they become part of your normal way of thinking and seeing the world; this operates in the same way that negative self-talk does, but in a way that benefits you.

To come up with your own positive affirmations, use the following guidelines:

What are your intentions? Think about what you are trying to create in your life. What does your dream life look like? Envision the behaviors, attitudes and traits you would like to develop. Would you like to live more peacefully? Would you like to practice healthier eating habits? Would you like to be a more supportive friend? You might want to write in a journal and brainstorm to figure out what's important to you and get to the heart of what you want to create in your life.

How do you say it? Once you get an idea of what you're aiming for, try to put that idea into a few simple statements that reflect the reality of what you want to create. Phrase the statements as if they are already true, not that you would like them to be true. For example, the affirmation, "I am feeling more peaceful each day," would be better than, "I want to feel more peaceful." This is because you are programming your subconscious mind to believe the statements, which helps manifest them into reality. You're not trying to want something; you're trying to make it happen.

When making positive affirmations, be sure they're positive! This means saying what you want to see and experience, not what you don't want to see and experience. For example, instead of saying, "I don't want to feel stress," or even, "I've stopped feeling stress," say, "I'm feeling peace." Often your subconscious mind doesn't register the negative and it just hears the word "stress"—which is what you're trying to avoid!

Once you've found your affirmations, here are some fun ways to introduce positive affirmations into your life:

Repetition: Probably the most popular way to harness the power of affirmations is to simply repeat them on a regular basis. Repeating them mentally several times in the morning or evening can be effective; repeating them out loud is even more effective because you register them more clearly that way.

Do-it-yourself recording: You can make a recording of yourself repeating positive affirmations and play it as you drive, wash dishes or get dressed in the morning. Talk in a calm voice, maybe play your favorite soothing music in the background, and you'll have a recording tailor-made especially for your needs! I first started playing with this many years ago. I made a recording of my voice saying all kinds of positive goals and I set it to go off by a timer instead of an alarm clock in the morning: "Wake up Jeffrey, you're a great chiropractor and everybody loves you." But I knew the technique had backfired for me the day I smashed the tape recorder to pieces. I'm not a morning person.

Write it on Post-its: A fun way to use affirmations is to write them down on sticky notes and tag them around your house (on the fridge, on the bathroom mirror and other places you'll likely see them). This will give you positive reminders throughout the day.

Examples of Stress Free Affirmations

I am strong.

I cope well and get on with my life during times of stress.

I think thoughts that uplift and nurture me.

I enjoy thinking positive thoughts that make me feel good about my life and myself.

I deserve to feel good right now.

I feel peaceful and calm.

My breathing is slow and calm.

My muscles are relaxed and comfortable.

I think through the solutions to my emotional issues slowly and peacefully.

I am thankful for all the positive things in my life.

I practice relaxation methods that I enjoy.

My body is healthy and strong.

I eat a well-balanced and nutritious diet.

I enjoy eating delicious and healthy food.

I do regular exercise that I enjoy.

I am filled with energy, vitality and self-confidence.

I am pleased with how I handle my emotional needs.

I know exactly how to manage my daily schedule to promote my emotional and physical well-being.

I listen to my body's needs and regulate my activity level to take care of those needs.

I love and honor my body.

I fill my mind with positive and self-nourishing thoughts.

I deserve health, vitality, and peace of mind.

I have total confidence in my ability to heal myself.

I feel radiant with abundant energy and vigor.

I appreciate the positive people and situations currently in my life.

I have a wonderful love life (don't laugh!).

I have a 31-inch waist (yeah right!).

VII. CREATE A PEACEFUL ENVIRONMENT

> "A CRUST EATEN IN PEACE IS BETTER THAN A BANQUET PARTAKEN
> IN ANXIETY." — AESOP, GREEK STORYTELLER

In these hectic times, it often seems we're rushing to and from activities, jobs, appointments and errands. How do we decompress and slow down the pace of our lives so we can face the next wave of responsibilities calmly? We can start by creating a peaceful haven within our homes. Your house should be a place where you feel safe and at ease, a place where daily renewal is not only a practice but a necessity.

One of the most important aspects of renewal is quiet. When our environment is quiet, our nervous systems have a chance to process all that comes our way during the day. It also allows you to plan and recharge for the next set of endeavors.

Your first step to creating a tranquil living environment is to de-clutter the main room where you and your family spend the most time. Clutter can be agitating and visually over-stimulating. Throw away the junk and organize the possessions you cherish. Be honest with yourself about what stuff you really need and enjoy! Donate to charity what you no longer wish to keep. Burn a sage smudge stick to chase away evil spirits.

Now you're ready to take the next steps:

> Your Television: Most people use TV to escape from reality. So some television can be relaxing, like some wine can be relaxing. But too much TV (or too much wine) can waste your time, eventually causing other forms of stress. So experiment and figure out the right amount of TV for you. And watch the right shows—if you watch violence before you go to bed you may have nightmares.

- Light candles: There's nothing more soothing than looking at the warm glow of a candle with its gentle flicker. Place a few in the room you use the most and enjoy the ambiance they create. Remember to keep candles out of the reach of pets and children and to blow them out when you're not around. If you set the house on fire, that's very bad.

- Keep the activity level low (unless you're having sex): Especially in the evening, it is important to slow things down. As a family, play board games, read, play cards or have poetry readings. Activities like these are a social alternative to zoning out in front of the television and can help everyone unwind from a busy day.

- Practice aromatherapy: Buy a diffuser at a local health food store, pour some water in it, put 2-3 drops of lavender oil in the water and then light the candle underneath. Lavender is a calming essential oil and works well to quiet the nervous system. Sniffing your loved ones can also be therapeutic.

- Bring nature into your home: Have houseplants in various areas of your home. Green plants cleanse the air and provide a constant flow of oxygen. They also soothe the soul – the color green has been shown to have a calming effect. Display fresh flowers whenever possible. Plants absorb negative energy, and colors of all kinds lift the mood and please the eyes.

- Limit computer time: Being on the computer is a big temptation for many people and often a necessity for doing research, writing papers or communicating with friends. But at times, it can be a real time-eater, like TV. Though it's not noisy like a TV, a computer can pull people away from each other. In the evenings, try to bring family members together in one room for a quiet activity. This increases conversation time, allows for sharing and ultimately creates tighter family bonds.

Turn off the ringer: Cherish family time, especially during mealtimes! When family members are sitting together having a meal or an important conversation, there's nothing more distracting than the phone ringing. Silence ringers. Voicemails can wait, but time together as a family is too precious to put off.

Use room-darkening techniques: Turn down the lights (dimmer switches are great for this), adjust the blinds or use sheer curtains to filter strong sunlight. Dimmed light signals that "quiet time" has begun.

Use artwork as a window to tranquility: Place art that you enjoy on your walls. Notice how it makes you feel: peaceful, happy, contemplative, calm. Remember, everyone who comes into your home will see it, so choose art that is conducive to a peaceful environment.

THE MUSIC SOLUTION

Music is a great way to help you to relax, relieve stress and ease anxieties. It also helps you function better mentally and physically, which is why music can be such effective therapy. It's regularly used during meditation and Tai Chi, and as an aid for sleep disorders. Music that has a tempo of 60 beats per minute works in synchrony with the human heartbeat, creating a naturally relaxing effect. It can slow the heart rate, breathing rate and thinking rate, and allow you to deepen into relaxation. Studies have suggested that slow, gentle, soothing music improves learning, creativity and memory. Music has such a powerful impact on people that it's used in many hospitals, clinics, schools, nursing homes and psychiatric hospitals to calm and revitalize both body and spirit.

A study published in *The Journal of Advanced Nursing* shows that listening to music actually reduces pain. The study, conducted at John Hopkins University, found that listening to soothing music for just an hour a day can lessen pain and reduce the depression associated with chronic pain.

As you embark on creating a soothing home for yourself and your family members, think about what helps you feel renewed and calm. It may be as simple as placing a potted plant on a windowsill or sitting quietly with distractions kept at bay. Whatever changes you make, ultimately you are also teaching your children how to find peace in the midst of a fast-paced world, and that's a skill they can use for a lifetime.

VIII. SLEEP: THE ULTIMATE FORM OF RELAXATION

> "STRESS IS WHEN YOU WAKE UP SCREAMING AND REALIZE YOU HAVEN'T FALLEN ASLEEP YET." —ANONYMOUS

For hundred of thousands of years, humans tended to go to sleep when it was dark and wake up when it was light. So, how long is it dark each night? Do you get that amount of sleep? I didn't think so.

Getting the right amount of quality sleep is vital to physical and mental health. Without it, your energy is drained and your mental sharpness dulls. Not getting enough sleep, or sleeping poorly due to sleep disorders, also increases the risk of accidents while driving or on the job. Symptoms often attributed to stress, aging or existing illnesses may in fact be due to sleep problems.

Sleep and rest are essential for a healthy life-balance. Enjoying a good night's sleep is not an extravagance; it's imperative for keeping your mind and body in working order. Basically, the more stress you're under and the more morons you have to deal with, the more sleep you'll need.

Our ancestors' sleep patterns were governed by and attuned to nature. We are born with genes and bodies which reflect our successful evolutionary survival over tens of thousands of years. Our genes and bodies do not reflect the modern world's less natural way of life.

Only in very recent generations have the modern heating, lighting, communications and entertainment technologies enabled (and encouraged) people to keep unnatural waking and working hours. Such behavior is truly at odds with our genetic preferences.

Resisting and breaking with our genetically-programmed sleep patterns creates internal conflicts and stresses, just as if we were to eat unnatural foods or breathe polluted air.

Napping during the day is also healthy. It recharges, relaxes and helps wipe the brain clean of pressures and unpleasant feelings. Research has shown that people who take a siesta of any frequency or duration are a third less likely to die of heart disease. The correlation between naps and heart health has also been found to be strongest for working men.

It can be tempting to put off sleep in favor of more work or socializing time, but when we do this, we pay with our health. And the consequences can result in serious health problems:

Weight gain and obesity

A study from the University of Chicago found that lack of sleep makes you want to eat more. Sleep loss appears to trigger changes in the hormones that regulate appetite. Not getting a full night's sleep stimulates hunger for high-calorie foods like cookies and chips. Researchers believe that we crave high-calorie foods when we're tired because they give us instant energy. According to a Columbia University study, people who get less than the recommended seven to eight hours of sleep a night are up to 73 percent more likely to be obese.

Cardiovascular health, cancer and diabetes

According to a Harvard-run Nurses' Health Study, failing to get enough sleep or sleeping at odd hours heightens the risk for a variety of major illnesses, including heart disease, cancer and diabetes. A report from the study summarizes that sleep deficit may put the body into a state of high alert, increasing the production of stress hormones and driving up blood pressure, a major risk factor for heart attacks and strokes. Additionally, people who are sleep-deprived have elevated levels of substances in the blood that indicate a heightened state of inflammation in the body, which is now also recognized as a major risk factor for heart disease, stroke, cancer and diabetes.

Depression and mood disorders

It's well-known that sleep problems can be a key sign of depression. However, the latest medical research now reports that the reverse is also true: sleep disorders can actually trigger depression or other mood disorders. Why? Sleep, mood and mental/emotional behaviors all share a complex mix of chemistry in the brain. Disordered sleep appears to set off a chain reaction of forces in the brain and nervous system that can result in a depressed mood, major depressive episode or other mood disorder.

Mental function and job performance

According to a Better Sleep Council survey, sleep-deprived workers reported the following as the work-related consequences of sleep loss:

- 31 percent reported a decline in the quality of their work.
- 31 percent reported impaired thinking or judgment at work.
- 30 percent reported trouble retaining information.
- The survey concluded, "sleep deprivation impacts your alertness, your productivity and your ability to socially interact with co-workers."

What is a sleep disorder?

More than 80 sleep disorders have been identified. It is estimated that 30 million Americans suffer from chronic sleep disorders, while an additional 40 million suffer from intermittent sleep problems. Those affected have problems ranging from not being able to sleep at all to being too sleepy to function during waking hours. Most adults need seven to eight hours of sleep per night to function optimally, though some people need less or more than that amount. When what seems like a sufficient amount of sleep doesn't leave you feeling refreshed, or you're still inexplicably tired, you may have a sleep disorder.

WHAT CAUSES SLEEP DEPRIVATION?

Not allowing enough time for sleep

Excessive worry, depression

Sleep disorders

Repeated awakenings from noise

Working at night, split shift work

Illnesses that cause chronic pain, difficulty breathing, etc.

Ways to Sleep Longer and Better at Night

Try to keep a regular bedtime and rising time in the morning, even on weekends and other days off from work. A regular sleeping pattern strengthens the sleep/wake cycle.

Avoid coffee, cola, tea, chocolate, alcohol and tobacco after supper.

Avoid heavy evening meals. A light snack or warm milk before bedtime may promote sleep.

Wind down for a period before sleep time. Quiet activities, such as reading, relaxing in a hot bath, prayer or meditating help promote sleep.

- Avoid using the bed as a place for watching television, doing paper work, eating or other activities. Bedrooms should be used only for sleeping and (if you're lucky!) sexual activity.

- If sleep does not occur after 30 minutes in bed, get up and engage in a quiet activity until sleepy. Do not watch television. A brief, slow walk may help.

- Avoid taking naps during the day, especially in the evening. If you must nap, do so in the early afternoon for no longer than 30 minutes.

- Check the bedroom temperature. Too hot or too cold temperatures interfere with sleep. Reducing the noise level is also helpful in creating an environment conducive to sleep.

- Engage in gentle exercise to produce fatigue before sleep. Heavy exercise should be avoided just before retiring because it tends to have an energizing effect.

- Schedule daily exposure to outdoor sunlight, especially in the late afternoon.

- Keep evening lights as low as possible for a few hours before bedtime.

- Restrict fluids in the evening and before retiring to help reduce the frequency of getting up to go to the bathroom.

- Indulge in a hot bath. Warm water loosens muscles, deepens respiration and relieves tension. A 30-minute soak right before bed can relax you and lighten worries, helping you fall asleep more easily.

CONTACT YOUR DOCTOR if your sleep does not improve after following these tips.

EXPRESSIONS FOR HIGH STRESS DAYS:

1. You! Off my planet!!
2. Not the brightest crayon in the box now, are we?
3. Well, this day was a total waste of makeup.
4. Errors have been made. Others will be blamed.
5. I'm not crazy. I've just been in a very bad mood for 28 years.
6. Allow me to introduce my selves.
7. Sarcasm is just one more service we offer.
8. Whatever kind of look you were going for, you missed.
9. Do they ever shut up on your planet?
10. I'm just working here till a good fast-food job opens up.
11. I'm trying to imagine you with a personality.
12. Stress is when you wake up screaming and you realize you haven't fallen asleep yet.
13. I can't remember if I'm the good twin or the evil one.
14. I just want revenge. Is that so wrong?
15. You say I'm a witch like it's a bad thing.
16. Nice perfume. Must you marinate in it?
17. Chaos, panic & disorder - my work here is done.
18. Everyone thinks I'm psychotic, except for my friends deep inside the earth.

19. Earth is full. Go home.
20. Is it time for your medication or mine?
21. Aw, did I step on your poor little bitty ego?
22. How do I set the laser printer to stun?
23. I'm not tense, just terribly, terribly alert.
24. When I want your opinion, I'll give it to you.

CHAPTER 4

DE-STRESS WITH CHIROPRACTIC CARE

An out-of-alignment spine pinches nerves and is the number one reason your body doesn't do what it's supposed to do. And guess what? Stress is one of the biggest contributors to spinal misalignment. Look at all your friends – they're all stressed out and messed up, and it's hard not to believe that being messed up is the way the human body is put together.

Well, it's not.

Your body is put together by all the wisdom in the universe to last ideally for 114 years. So, why are we hobbling around with all this sickness and disease? Why are we lining up for medication and unnecessary surgery? Why are people in their fifties, sixties and seventies feeling so achy and headed for nursing homes or even death? Because most people walk around for part or most of their lives with spines out of alignment, with twisted vertebrae pinching nerves.

If you've got pinched nerves, you can never be truly healthy. Unaligned backbones make you extra-susceptible to aches and ailments. You'll be tired and irritable, you'll suffer stomach–and backaches, and when you get those X-rays back from the doctor, you'll say, "Arthritis? But I'm only fifty!" And people will tell you, "Well, you're getting older."

But it doesn't have to be like that! Fifty isn't old. Fifty is only the halfway point. You shouldn't have a serious problem with arthritis in your joints until you're extremely old or unless you're genetically prone to it.

Remember that your spine has probably been out of alignment since childhood. All the sitting you've done over the years, the falls, the accidents, the injuries – all of it adds up, so most adults need to come in for at corrective chiropractic care to get the spine realigned, strengthened and rehabilitated. Once your spine is back to normal, periodic treatments

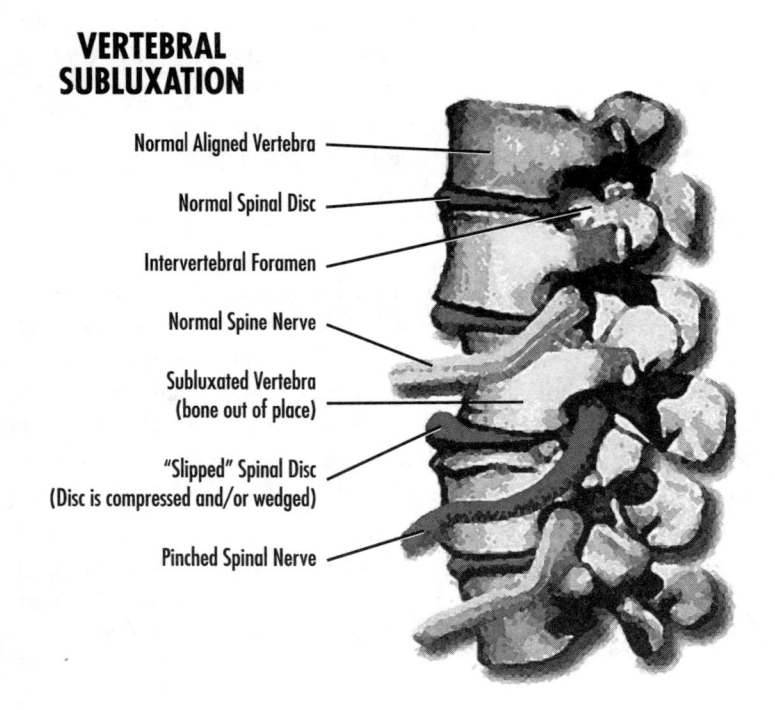

VERTEBRAL SUBLUXATION

- Normal Aligned Vertebra
- Normal Spinal Disc
- Intervertebral Foramen
- Normal Spine Nerve
- Subluxated Vertebra (bone out of place)
- "Slipped" Spinal Disc (Disc is compressed and/or wedged)
- Pinched Spinal Nerve

after that will undo the stresses that you do to keep your spine in line so that you can be healthy and live as long as possible.

Let me tell you what will happen if you don't treat your spine right. Many patients come in for chiropractic appointments long enough to get rid of their pain and get patched up. We mark their files "Relief Only." They come in whenever they hurt. But they don't actually get the problem corrected. They don't strengthen their spine or get on a reliable rehabilitation program they can do on their own time. So, the problem comes back again. Here's the thing: As their bones go in and out of alignment, the discs wear out. The nerves start pinching into organ systems, setting the person up for disease.

In my opinion, it could be worse to be out of alignment than to smoke. Pinched nerves affect every cell, every tissue, every organ in the body – and you pay the price. When? When you're a little older. Younger bodies can take quite a bit of abuse, but eventually the damage will accumulate and catch up with you.

UNLOCKING THE INNER DOCTOR (Your Innate Intelligence!)

It's important to trust your own body to heal itself if you keep it in good shape. Ten percent of the population's spines are in alignment and 90 percent are not. Look on the positive side: at one point in your life, your spine was in alignment. When you injured yourself, your body cleared away the damaged tissues and replaced them. The power of your body to regenerate and rejuvenate itself is still there, you just need to unlock that power. Your body is your internal wisdom, your inborn doctor. That wisdom made your body, runs your body and heals your body. Right now your body is regulating its blood pressure, for example. Internal blood pressure mechanisms are designed by all the wisdom of the universe to work perfectly. Think of all the other parts of your body that are regenerating and rejuvenating you. Right now, your heart is beating and fighting off heart disease. Your lungs are breathing and keeping out all the bacteria, viruses, pollen and smoke. You'd be dead in 15 seconds if that system wasn't working.

The difference between your body fighting off disease and drugs fighting off disease is simple. Your body neutralizes the attack, while a drug carpet-bombs your body's immune system and leaves 14 pages of potential side effects in its wake. When your stomach gets too acidy, you say, "I must have a Tums deficiency." But antacids can only do so much. When your stomach hurts, your body's defense system is telling you that it's not intact. It needs readjustment. If your digesting system were in working order, it would digest and absorb the food in the way it was meant to be absorbed.

Your body came with its own user's manual. At one point, you were one cell. Remember that? Actually, you got half your chromosomes from Mom and half from Dad—twenty-four chromosomes from each came together to make one cell. Then what happened? The cell divided into two. Two becomes four. Four becomes eight. Eight becomes sixteen. Sixteen becomes thirty-two. Thirty-two becomes sixty-four. Sixty-four becomes one-hundred-twenty-eight. One-hundred-twenty-eight becomes…who cares! If I knew I'd tell you, but math isn't my subject. That's why I became a chiropractor. Okay, back to where babies come from: what happens next is your brain and spinal cord begins to develop. This initial growth is called the primitive streak. From the spinal cord, little branches grow, and organs begin to develop innate intelligence from the branches. Now, as you get older, your body still has this inborn intelligence telling your body what to do and how to heal itself. This intelligence regulates nerve flow, or impulses, and guess where most of that happens? In your spine. Those smart impulses runs from your brain down your spinal cord along your nerves to every cell, every tissues and every organ in your body. When you get a pinched nerve, this intelligent flow of information gets stuck. You could take drugs to mask the pain. Medication is great for killing pain. But so is tequila.

That's where chiropractic treatment comes in: we serve tequila. Just kidding! Getting realigned allows those impulses to flow freely again and helps your body get back on track by working with it, not against it. The longer your spine is lined up correctly and the nerves are flowing, the better you will be able to fight off aging, disease and stress. Your body will heal itself faster and won't need as many medications to keep itself in working order.

Keeping your spine in line is just as important as saving up for retirement. In fact, maybe it's even more important: stay healthy, find a job that you enjoy and that helps others, keep doing it at least part time until you're 114 years old and then you can drop dead while you're doing it with your boots on and a smile on your face. Get that look off of your face; you'll be 114 years old. It will be time to die. People who stop producing, providing and participating are more likely to become disabled.

Keeping your spine in good shape for life takes a long time and a lot of treatments. But you'll reap the benefits into old age. When you're a spry 93, you'll be playing hoops in your backyard with the neighbors like a pro. Hey, you never know.

HOW CHIROPRACTIC TREATMENT WORKS

A Canadian-turned-Iowan named Dr. Daniel David Palmer developed chiropractic spine manipulation in the late 1800s. He theorized that every human had an innate intelligence that coursed through the spinal column and controlled the body's functions using the nervous system. When the spinal column doesn't line up just right (called a "subluxation"), he believed this has a direct impact on overall health: ninety-five percent of nerve interference can be traced to misaligned spines, while the other five percent are caused by other joint issues.

What sets chiropractic care apart from mainstream medicine is that it works in a non-invasive, cooperative way with your body instead of against it. Chiropractic treatment approaches your health in a holistic way. Your health is more than charts and numbers; a chiropractor takes your lifestyle, environment and emotions into account when evaluating your wellbeing. As a result, many patients feel empowered and more in control of their own health after visiting a chiropractor. Especially a chiropractor like me.

If you know what's going on in your spine at the structural and nerve level, you'll better understand why your back is hurting and how this affects your entire body. Twenty-four small bones called vertebrae make up your spinal column. Seven of these bones are in your neck, twelve are in the mid-back and five are in the lower back. These vertebrae stack one on top of the other. When you look at them from front to back, they should form a straight line. Most people don't have perfectly aligned spines. The vertebrae may be twisted or rotated, or the spine might veer slightly to the left or to the right.

When your spine isn't aligned, the nerves signals can't get through your spinal column efficiently. The flow of messages from your brain out to your limbs gets distorted, often undermining body processes or causing disease. This is called "nerve interference." Think of it like interference on a radio station: the signal gets scrambled and you don't get a clear transmission. But unlike hearing static on a radio with interference, most people don't immediately notice when or where they have nerve interference. Years can go by without a person noticing the ill effects of cramped vertebrae.

When I talk about nerve flow, I'm essentially referring to the flow of electricity through your body. According to research conducted by Harvard orthopedist Joel Goldthwaite, how the body works electrically and how the components of electricity flow through the body change

SPINAL VERTEBRAE

Cervical Spine (Neck)

Thoracic Spine (Mid-back)

Lumbar Spine (Low back)

Sacrum & Coccyx (Pelvis)

SPINAL NERVES	AREAS AND PARTS OF BODY	POSSIBLE SYMPTOMS
1C	Back of the head	Headaches (including migraines), aches or pains at the back of the head, behind the eyes or in the temples, tension across the forehead, throbbing or pulsating discomfort at the top or back of head
2C	Various areas of the head	
3C	Side and front of the neck	
4C	Upper back of neck	
5C	Middle of neck and upper part of arms	Jaw muscle or joint aches or pains
6C	Lower part of neck, arms, and elbows	Dizziness, nervousness, vertigo
7C	Lower part of arms, shoulders	Soreness, tension and tightness in back of neck and throat areas
1T	Hands, wrists, fingers, thyroid	Pain, soreness, and restriction in the shoulder area
2T	Heart, it's valves and coronary arteries	Bursitis, tendonitis
3T	Lungs, bronchial tubes, pleura, chest	Pain and soreness in arms, hands, elbows and/or fingers
4T	Gall bladder, common duct	Chest pains, tightness or constriction
5T	Liver, solar plexes	Asthma, difficult breathing
6T	Stomach, mid-back area	Middle or lower mid-back pain, discomfort and soreness
7T	Pancreas, duodenum	Various and numerous symptons from trouble or malfunctioning of
8T	Spleen, lower mid-back	Thyroid
9T	Adrenal glands	Heart
		Lungs
10T	Kidneys	Gall bladder
		Liver
11T	Ureters	Stomach
		Pancreas
12T	Small intestines, upper/lower back	Spleen
		Adrenal glands
		Kidneys
1L	Iliocecal valve, large intestines	Small and large intestines
		Sex organs
2L	Appendix, abdomen, upper leg	Uterus
		Bladder
3L	Sex organs, uterus, bladder, knees	Prostate glands
4L	Prostate gland, lower back	Low back pain, aches and soreness
		Trouble walking
5L	Sciatic nerve, lower legs, ankles, feet	Leg, knee, ankle and foot soreness and pain
Sacrum	Hip bones, buttocks	Sciatica, pain or soreness in the hip and buttocks
Coccyx	Rectum, anus	Rectal trouble

the way the entire body functions. Goldthwaite discovered that he was able to cure many chronic health problems by getting people to exist and function more symmetrically. This, of course, is one of the main ideas behind chiropractic spinal manipulations: getting your body aligned and in symmetry. According to Goldthwaite, if you're not properly aligned, electrical flow shorts out and scrambled messages get sent back and forth from brain to nerve ending. Then sooner or later you get pain or numbness or tingling or weakness.

But most of your nervous system travels inside to the organs. And if the nerves are interfered to your insides, the cell and tissues inside of you start heading for disease. Your nerves control the glands that make up your body chemistry. So, with subluxations (nerve interference) to your glands, you become susceptible to headaches, dizziness, blurred vision, depression, fatigue, and difficulties in concentration and sleep.

YOUR FIRST APPOINTMENT

A lot of people are intimidated the first time they walk into my office and they see the table. They think I'm going to start crunching their backs right away. And they're thinking, "Oh no, you don't. You're not gonna touch my head like that. Arnold Schwarzenegger does that and he kills a guy." Well, as a matter of fact, Arnold Schwarzenegger is into chiropractic treatment. He's been adjusted at least once a week for I don't know how long. Who adjusts him, you ask? His friend and Italian bodybuilder-turned-chiropractor Dr. Franco Columbu.

When you go in for your initial appointment, relax. Before a chiropractor can start adjusting, he or she has to really understand where you as a patient are coming from, what your medical history is and how you're feeling.

The chiropractor then evaluates you for the presence of nerve interference. This part of the evaluation is usually conducted using an examination technique called palpation. The doctor carefully feels your entire spinal region for signs of nerve interference. A series of orthopedic, neurological, physical and chiropractic tests are performed to determine the cause of your health problem and the best method of getting you well. X-rays may also be used to detect the physical signs of nerve impingement: soft tissue damage to nerves, muscles or discs.

After the doctor has studied your spine, health history and X-rays, he or she will meet with you to discuss the results and the recommended course of chiropractic care. The doctor can also explain in depth how each part of the spine corresponds to and serves a certain portion of the body and its organs.

Once the chiropractor has located your nerve interference, he or she applies pressure on the culprit vertebrae to help it push off the nerve. In fact, chiropractic is Greek for "done by hand." The first adjustment begins to restore the vertebra to its natural position, so these tissues must have time to "rehabilitate." That's why a series of adjustments are needed to get you on the road back to health.

It's important to remember that the chiropractor isn't forcing the twisted vertebrae back into place. Instead, the body is getting adjusted so that it can fix its own nerve interference. In a way, the chiropractor is simply removing the interference so your body's inner intelligence can get back to work.

CONTINUING YOUR CHIROPRACTIC TREATMENT

After enough adjustments, many patients say they feel peaceful and relaxed, enjoy better sleep and have increased energy. Other patients report feeling discomfort ranging from headaches to general fatigue. But with continued adjustments, these feelings go away and most people feel much better.

What's happening here is that your spinal nerves, pinched and under stress for years and years, are suddenly coming back to life. As they heal, they're often sensitive. Pains from injuries that happened years ago may resurface as your body finally heals. This is called "retracing." Your body tissue has a collective memory which records and remembers all the traumas, injuries and accidents it has experienced. So, when you begin healing after a chiropractic adjustment, your body sometimes re-experiences the feelings from an old injury. Sometimes retracing is almost imperceptible, but for some people it can be so intense that they feel worse rather than better. Be patient if this happens. If you stop getting adjustments, you may be cheating yourself out of a full recovery.

Most patients will begin to feel better in a relatively short period of time. To correct, strengthen, rehabilitate, mobilize and make the spine function as close to 100 percent as possible takes a long time and a lot of treatments—as much as six to eight months of treatments, followed by weekly or monthly treatments once your body has begun to heal itself. This should undo whatever it is you are doing to yourself and keep you as normal as possible.

Like orthodontist fixes your teeth, chiropractors fix your spine. How long does it take the orthodontist to straighten your teeth?

And how often should you go? It's similar to exercise, the more often you go, the better the results.

MOST COMMON REASONS PEOPLE SEEK OUT CHIROPRACTIC CARE

1. Backaches
2. Neck aches
3. Pain, numbness, tingling in the arms or legs.

4. Headaches
5. Fatigue
6. Dizziness
7. Trouble sleeping
8. Carpal Tunnel
9. Internal Disorders
10. Depression or Moodiness

Should you be experiencing any of these symptoms, don't wait! Make an appointment with a chiropractor today. Keep in mind that subluxations can manifest as many different problems. So if you don't feel well, first check with your chiropractor.

CRUNCHING NUMBERS

Of the nearly 30,000 people I have treated over almost three decades, the ones surveyed report that:

- 71 percent take less medication
- 87 percent experienced an improvement in their overall health
- 92 percent are living healthier lives
- 93 percent saw an improvement in physical problems
- 91 percent experienced a decrease in physical pain
- 90 percent who were headed for surgery didn't have it

Do you think people under medical care get these kinds of results?

Stress and Your Spine

Many factors can lead to twisted vertebrae and pinched nerves, but stress is especially hard on your spine. What do you do when you worry? You scrunch up your shoulders. What do you do when you're stressed out at work? Well, most people tend to hunch their backs or slouch, especially when in front of a computer. Emotional stress often manifests itself in poor posture and tense muscles.

Next time you feel stressed, make a careful mental evaluation of how your body is feeling. How are you sitting? How are you walking? Are your shoulders scrunched up? Is your back straight or hunched over?

Having an aligned spine can have a profound effect on your mood productivity and your energy.

Don't be fooled, however. The "popping" noises your back makes when you twist or stretch don't necessarily mean you're correcting your spine's nerve interference. Often vertebrae "pop" but don't actually move out of their twisted positions. Only a chiropractor knows the exact technique and force necessary to fix your spinal nerve flow. Chiropractic treatment is definitely not a "Do It Yourself" endeavor.

But it's still very important to stretch your spine regularly and keep it strong – just do so in an informed and healthy way. If you develop a personal exercise regimen, you'll be one big step closer to eliminating needless stress in your life.

Strengthening Your Back during Everyday Activities

You don't necessarily need to drop a lot of money on a gym membership or spend hours every day on a training machine to get the benefits of good exercise for you spine. You can easily incorporate simple back-strengthening exercises into your daily life. Even simple movements—like rolling your shoulders or pulling in your abdominal muscles—have a profound, long-lasting effect on your back strength if you do them regularly. The good news is that you can do these exercises just about anywhere, anytime.

Before you get out of bed in the morning...

Push your head with force against your pillow and hold for six seconds. It's a great wake-up tonic. Pretty soon you won't even need coffee!

Grab your arm above the wrist and squeeze for six seconds

As you get up, sitting on the edge of your bed...

Put your hands on your knees and push down.

Put the palm of your right hand against the inside of your left knee and the palm of the left hand against the inside of the right knee. Push your hands against your knees while resisting with the knees.

Once you're up...

Stand about two feet from the wall and crouch slightly so that your knees are bent and the heels are off the floor. Lean forward with your palms against the wall and fingers up. Now push with your whole body's strength.

In the bathroom...

As you shave, wash, brush your teeth, put on lipstick (if you're a female. If you're a guy putting on lipstick...well, I wouldn't recommend that. Not that there is anything wrong with that, you freak): pull in those abdominal muscles and hold them as hard as you can. Get in the habit of starting the day with your stomach held in.

Try a soundless scream. Open your mouth and eyes as wide as you possibly can, stretching the muscles against the skin and bone that hold your face together. Try to tear your face apart!

Then, try to squeeze your face together, from top to bottom, making it as small and scrunched-up as you possibly can.

While driving...

At traffic lights, pull in your abdominal muscles as hard as you can and hold for six seconds.

Place your hands on the outside of the steering wheel and push, then pull. Try this while holding in your abdominal muscles.

Reach your arms overhead and push against the roof of the car.

Place hands on knees, then push down with all the muscles of your forearms, upper arms, shoulders and chest while pushing up from the toes, using the muscles of your thighs and abdomen.

While waiting for a bus, taxi or elevator (or wherever there's a wall, post or doorway)...

Face the wall, reach up and place your hands on the top ledge and pull down.

Squeeze a post, trying to push it away from you or to one side or the other.

Stand sideways next to a structure or wall and push your arm against it, trying to raise your arm straight up through it.

Stand with your side to a wall and push your leg or foot against it, trying to raise them.

Stand with your back to a wall, trying to push your heel back through it.

Put your toe against a wall and push with all your strength.

On the telephone...

Grip the phone and squeeze with all your might.

Grip the phone with one hand on the mouthpiece and the other on the earphone and try to tear it apart.

Hold the phone in front of you and try to push it together.

Use your phone as a timing device for other isometric exercises. Don't answer the first ring. Start any convenient exercise at the conclusion of the first ring and hold it during the interval between rings.

While talking on the phone, put a wastepaper basket or book between your feet. With legs out straight, squeeze in against it, using your leg muscles from the hips down.

Place the ball of your left foot on the toes of your right foot. Push down with the left foot from the ankle while pulling up with your right. Repeat on the other side.

Keeping Your Spine Healthy

If you're following a treatment program with a chiropractor, it's still important to be good to your back. Don't think, "Oh, the chiropractor will take care of that." Chiropractors like to practice what's called "active care." This is treatment that asks you to take responsibility for your own recovery into your own hands – through exercise, ergonomics and lifestyle changes. The more aware you are of what does your back good and how you can protect it, the faster you'll recover and the faster your body's inner intelligence will start taking care of you.

Follow these simple tips to maintain an aligned back when you're lifting heavy objects:

Never bend from the waist only. Instead, bend from the hips and knees.

Never lift a heavy object higher than your waist.

Always turn and face the object you wish to lift.

Don't twist and lift.

Avoid carrying unbalanced loads and hold heavy objects close to your body.

Never carry anything heavier than you can manage with ease.

Never lift or move heavy furniture. Wait for someone to do it who knows the principles of leverage.

Avoid sudden movements and sudden "overloading" of muscles. Learn to move deliberately, swinging the legs from the hips.

Learn to keep the head in line with the spine, when standing, sitting and lying in bed.

Put soft chairs and deep couches on your "don't sit" list. If you must sit for a long time, cross your legs at the ankles to rest your back.

Borrow or buy a rocking chair. Rocking rests the back by changing the muscle groups your body uses.

Train yourself vigorously to use your abdominal muscles to flatten your lower abdomen. In time, this muscle contraction will become habitual, making you look and feel better.

For good posture, concentrate on strengthening the abdominal and buttock muscles.

Sleep on your side or back.

Especially for women:

Wear shoes with moderate heels, all about the same height. Avoid changing from high to low heels.

Avoid carrying a purse that is too heavy.

Especially for men:

Wear supportive shoes. When heels and soles are worn, replace them.

Do not sit on a large wallet. Remove when sitting or carry a money clip. Just give the large wallet to your woman. Why not? It saves time.

CHAPTER 5

THE EXERCISE AND NUTRITION SOLUTION

MOVE IT OR LOSE IT!

In my 27 years as a practicing chiropractor, I've treated over 26,000 people for backaches, neck pain, headaches, fatigue, depression and other health problems. The ones who have the most severe problems and the ones who have the hardest time recuperating are the people who sit all day. Excessive sitting causes the body and the spine to get weak and stiff. Humans are not designed to sit all day long! Our bodies are built to move, so it's no wonder that avoiding it creates all kinds of discomfort and tension. In fact, the more your exercise, the less stress-related physical symptoms you'll experience.

Both muscle-building and stamina-building exercise relaxes tense muscles and tight connective tissues, the first parts of the body to show the strains of stress. Ask anyone who's just finished a long walk or a game of soccer if they feel at all stressed. Of course they don't.

Something terrific happens in the brain when the body works out, especially aerobic exercise: your heart starts pumping and it pumps the worries and tenseness right out of your body!

In this section we'll discuss some of the basic facts about exercise and why you need to exercise frequently to keep yourself de-stressed and healthy. Exercise, like a healthier diet, isn't complicated to understand-- the answers are simple, the opportunity is there—it's the personal commitment that makes the difference.

Research has shown that physical exercise is an excellent tension reliever. Quite simply, nothing eases stress more than exercise. Even better, exercise improves your cardiovascular functions by strengthening and enlarging the heart, causing greater elasticity of the blood vessels, increasing oxygen throughout your body and lowering your blood levels of fats such as bad cholesterol and triglycerides. All of this, of course, means less chance of developing heart conditions, strokes or high blood pressure.

Exercise attacks stress on two sides: first, it produces positive biochemical changes in the body and brain that improve your mood; second, it takes your mind off your problems by resting and renewing the nerve cells in the brain that fuel tension and worry. In addition, many kinds of strenuous exercise provide an outlet for negative emotions such as frustration, anger and irritability. It's hard to feel angry or irritable after you've punched a boxing bag or kicked a field goal!

Even regular, low-impact exercise reduces the amount of adrenaline and cortisol your body releases in response to stress. All exercise releases endorphins and serotonin, those powerful, pain-relieving, mood-elevating chemicals in the brain. A "runner's high," for example, is the result of a flood of endorphins rushing through the body post-run.

Even though exercise can be a great 'fix' for stress, it's not for everyone undergoing stress. For people who have a sedentary job or lifestyle, it could work wonders. For the person who is already physically overworked and drained, it simply doesn't make any sense to add additional physical strain. However, most Americans don't exercise enough.

But for most stressed people, the value of exercising at least three times a week for 20 to 60 minutes cannot be overemphasized.

AEROBIC VS. ANAEROBIC EXERCISE

The two types of exercise – aerobic and anaerobic—perform different functions. Aerobic exercise is sustained activity involving the major muscle groups, such as swimming, running or brisk walking. Your heart and respiratory rate increase, and more oxygen circulates through the body. This kind of exercise strengthens your cardiovascular system and increases overall strength and stamina. The goal of aerobic exercise is for your pulse to reach the training rate appropriate for your age. You must stay at the rate for at least twenty minutes and exercise at this level for a minimum of three times a week in order to reap the benefits of aerobic exercise.

"Low-impact," or anaerobic, exercise is less vigorous and doesn't maintain your training heart rate. But this doesn't mean low-impact exercise is useless! In fact, anaerobic exercise improves your muscle strength and flexibility and can still be a good outlet for letting go of bottled-up feelings.

There are three kinds of anaerobic exercise:

> Isotonics require your muscles to contract against a resistant object with movement, such as in weight lifting.
>
> Isometrics require that your muscles contract against resistance without movement, thereby increasing strength without building bulk.

Calisthenics are stretching exercises, such as sit-ups, toe touches and knee-bends, and help increase flexibility and joint mobility

What kind of exercise you choose depends on your physical ability as well as your preferences. The most important rule is to choose activities that you enjoy and that are accessible and feasible for you to do regularly. You should also consider whether you want to make your exercise routine a social activity or a personal time when you can be alone with your thoughts. Some people find that exercising with others provides them with a web of support and encouragement, while others prefer the calming effects of exercising alone with music or in silence. I enjoy listening to self-help books on tape while I lift weights or walk.

Optimally exercise should be done at least five days each week. Just getting yourself moving is important, but making exercise a regular routine in your life will make it easier to incorporate into your life. The human body craves consistency and can make adjustments to long-term demands placed upon it. If you exercise three times per week, it will have a conditioning effect on your heart, but the heart is not the only part of your body that needs to perform efficiently during exercise. The other organs and muscle tissues will respond much differently to exercise five days in a row. For five days in a row the body continues to receive the message that it needs to perform efficiently in order to keep up, so it adjusts to meet the demand. As a result, your body runs an efficient operation of the whole system, all the time, even on the two days you don't exercise. Those five days of exercise should consist primarily of aerobic with intermittent bouts of anaerobic work. You should sustain the aerobic part of the workout about 20 to 60 minutes.

Some people gain weight due to stress and not because of increased food intake or reduction in activity levels. Combining regular, vigorous exercise along with eliminating stress can bring about a reversal: significant weight reduction.

While five days of regular, vigorous exercise stimulates efficiency throughout the body, too much vigorous exercise can cause the body to go into survival mode and cause damage. This is why it's vital that any exercise program starts off gradually and increases in intensity as your endurance improves.

Before you begin any exercise program, you should get a physical examination. If you are over the age of forty, your doctor will probably want to do a stress electrocardiogram to determine how much activity your heart can handle. If you have not exercised regularly for some time, begin slowly with low-impact exercise and gradually increase your activity. If you experience any adverse side effects, such as dizziness, cramps or chest pain, stop exercising and consult your physician.

A LOW IMPACT EXERCISE ROUTINE

Following is a basic low-impact exercise routine that you can do at home. Remember that this does not provide an aerobic workout—for that, you must choose an activity such as bicycling, running, brisk walking, swimming, aerobic dance or use a machine such as a stationary bicycle, Lifecycle, Stairmaster or treadmill. When you exercise, wear loose, comfortable clothing and supportive sneakers. Wait two hours after a meal before exercising in order to avoid cramping or nausea, and be sure to drink plenty of water before, during and after your workout.

Bestselling author Dr. Dean Ornish says that moderate exercise seems to be enough to make you healthy. He recommends only 30 minutes of walking or similar activities once a day (or an hour of walking three times a week). Dr. Andrew Weil (famous for popularizing integrative medicine) recommends a 45-minute brisk walk or its equivalent most days of the week.

Doctors vary a little in their exact recommendations for exercise, but the bottom line is clear: exercise is vital for well-being.

Warming Up (at least five minutes)

1. Stand with your feet shoulder-width apart, your arms at your sides. Gently roll your head in a half circle in front of you, back and forth a few times. With your head straight, drop your left ear to your shoulder and hold. Bring your head to center and drop your right ear to your shoulder and hold. Bring your head back up and drop your chin to your chest. Head up and drop it back. Bring your head back up and face forward.

2. Shrug your shoulders up and release; repeat six times. Roll your shoulders backward six times; roll them forward six times.

3. Place your left hand on your hip and raise your right arm up. Keeping your torso straight, reach your right arm over your head and bend to the left from your waist. Hold and then return to center. Repeat with the left arm reaching over your head to the right. You should feel a stretch in your sides.

4. Stand with your feet slightly more than shoulder-width apart. Reach down your left leg as far as you can, trying to touch your ankle or toes if possible. Hold for ten seconds. Slowly roll yourself upright, keeping your head down to avoid dizziness. Now reach down your right leg in the same manner and hold. Again, roll up slowly with your head down. This stretches the muscles in the backs of your legs.

5. Still standing with your feet apart, turn to your left. Bend your left knee and extend your right leg straight out behind you. Center your body so that your left knee is bent at a 90-degree angle to the floor. Hold this position, called a runner's stretch, for a count of ten, gently pressing your straight leg down toward the floor.

You'll feel the stretch in the thigh muscle of the out-stretched leg. Repeat this exercise with your right leg.

6. To stretch your Achilles tendon and calf muscles, stand two to three feet from a wall and place your hands on it. Keeping your legs straight and your feet flat on the floor, lean in to the wall. You should feel the stretch in your legs; hold it for ten seconds. Try stepping back a bit farther to increase the stretch, remembering that your feet should remain flat on the floor.

EXERCISING AND CONDITIONING (15-20 minutes)

With all of the following exercises, be sure to do the repetitions slowly and evenly, with some tension in your limbs. Your arms should not simply swing back and forth, but should move in a controlled, deliberate way, almost as if they were resisting against an invisible weight or moving through peanut butter.

All of these exercises suggest ten repetitions, but if you are just starting out, do as many as you feel comfortable doing. "No pain, no gain" may be true to some extent for accomplished athletes, but for the average person, pain often signals stress. Stay tuned to the sensations in your muscles and use common sense. If it hurts too much, it's time to stop. As you exercise, your muscle tissue actually breaks down. In order to allow your muscles time to restore themselves, work out every other day or exercise different body areas on alternating days.

ARMS

1. Stand with your feet shoulder-width apart, stomach tucked in, and back straight. Extend your arms out to the sides with you, palms facing out. Bring your arms in together straight out in front of you, palms out, and extend back out. Do ten repetitions.

2. Keeping your arms extended, bring them straight up together above your head and then drop them so that they extend out to the sides. Repeat ten times.

3. Arms still extended with palms facing out, move your arms forward in small circles. Do ten of these and then increase to a medium-size circle. Do ten repetitions and then ten more, making the largest circle you can. Repeat this cycle, moving your arms backward. Remember to move your arms deliberately and slowly.

4. Extend your arms out to the sides, bend them at the elbows, and make fists. Squeeze your bent arms together so that your forearms meet in front of you. This exercise works the chest and arms.

5. To work your biceps, extend your arms straight down at your sides with your inner forearms and fists facing up. Bending at the elbow, squeeze your fists to your shoulders. In order to obtain the maximum benefit, pretend there is a weight on your inner forearm and resist against the pressure as you squeeze up.

WAIST

1. Standing with your feet shoulder-width apart, bend to the left, reaching slightly down and out as far as you can with your left arm. Your right hand can remain on your hip or your elbow can rise up simultaneously as you are reaching to the side with your left arm. Do ten repetitions and then repeat with the right side.

2. Standing with your feet apart, place your hands on your hips or raise your arms to chest level and bend them at the elbows so that your forearms are directly in front of your chest. With straight hips, twist from the waist ten times to the left and ten times to the right. Then try alternating the movement, pausing in the forward position between each twist.

3. This one may be a little harder to do. Sit on the floor with your legs spread open as wide as possible and your hands clasped behind your head. Keeping your back straight and your elbows back, reach down toward the floor behind your left knee with your left elbow. Come up, pause, and then reach down toward the floor behind your right knee with your right elbow. Do ten repetitions.

ABDOMEN

1. Sit on the floor with your knees slightly bent and your back straight. You can hold your arms straight out in front of you for balance or you can cross them over your chest. From this sitting position, slowly roll back so that your shoulders are just a few inches above the floor. Pause and then slowly roll back up to a sitting position. As you do this exercise, always press the small of your back downward (rather than arching your back) to prevent strain. Do ten repetitions.

2. Lie on the floor with your stomach tucked in so that the small of your back presses down toward the floor. Bend your knees slightly and keep your feet flat on the floor. Clasp your hands behind your head, and, keeping your elbows back as much as possible, slowly raise your head and shoulders up off the ground. In order to help you do this exercise properly, pick a spot on the ceiling and raise your chin up toward that spot. Your head, neck, and shoulders should stay aligned and straight; you should not be "hunching" up, tucking your chin in, or using your elbows and arms to pull yourself up. If you don't do this exercise in the proper way, your abdomen will not benefit at all. If you do it properly, however, you will feel your abdominal muscles contract as you come up and relax as you come down. Do ten repetitions slowly and rhythmically.

3. Here is a more advanced form of exercise. Lying in the same position, rest your left leg on your right knee. Lift your head and shoulders up in the same manner as above. Do ten repetitions and then switch legs for ten more.

Thighs

Sit on the floor with your back straight, your hands on the floor to your sides and slightly behind you with your arms straight to support your body. Keeping your right leg relaxed, straighten your left leg, point your toe and slowly raise it up about a foot off the ground. Lower the leg and repeat ten times. Switch legs and repeat ten times with your right leg. Remember to keep your back straight as you do this exercise.

Inner Thighs

Sitting in the same position as in the previous exercise with your legs extended straight out in front of you, lift your left leg a few inches off the floor, point your toe and slowly move it out to the left. You'll feel a nice stretch on the inside of your thigh. Bring your leg back to the starting position and repeat ten times. Switch legs and repeat ten times with your right leg.

Outer Thighs

Lie on your left side, your left arm bent at the elbow so that your hand supports your head and your legs are stacked on top of each other. Make sure your back is straight with your pelvis tilted slightly toward the floor. Bend your bottom leg at the knee and keep this leg relaxed. Straighten your top leg, toe pointed, and raise it up as far as you can. You'll want to keep your leg straight as you raise it so that the outer thigh is parallel with the ceiling. Lower your leg and repeat ten times. When you do this exercise, pretend there is a weight on your outer thigh and resist against it as you raise your leg. This will maximize the benefit to your muscles. Do ten repetitions and then lie on your opposite side and work your opposite leg.

Buttocks

Lie on your back, your knees bent with your feet apart, your hands clasped behind your head or placed under your buttocks. Without arching your back, lift your buttocks off the floor. Squeeze your buttocks with each lift and then release as you come back to the floor. Do ten repetitions with your feet apart and then ten with your feet together. As you master this exercise, you can do it keeping your feet apart with your knees together or with your feet together and your knees spread apart. Those who are more advanced can cross one leg over the opposite knee and vice versa.

Cool Down

Using the stretches described in the warm-up, be sure to spend at least five minutes cooling down after your exercise routine. If you do aerobic exercise, cool down by slowing your pace for five minutes as well as doing five minutes of stretching exercises. For example, when you're done jogging or bicycling, take a brisk walk to cool down; if you swim, cool down by doing gentle breast-, back-, or sidestrokes for five minutes. Although you may be tempted sometimes to skip the stretching, remember that your muscles have contracted and tightened during exercise and they must be stretched out in order to prevent cramping and injuries, such as pulls.

RECOMMENDATIONS FOR DAILY AEROBIC EXERCISE

    Walking in the woods, at the beach or in the park
    Bicycling
    Yoga
    Tai Chi Chuan or some other form of martial arts
    Tennis, basketball, volleyball, racquetball or other group sport
    Boxing
    Jogging
    Dancing

Yoga 101

Dating back more than 5000 years, yoga is the oldest defined practice of self-development. The methods of classical yoga include ethical disciplines, physical postures, breathing control and meditation. Traditionally an Eastern practice, it's now becoming popular in the West. In fact, many business companies, especially in Britain, are recognizing the benefits of yoga and noticing that relaxed workers are healthier and more creative, so they're sponsoring yoga fitness programs for their employees.

Overview of Yoga

    Many of the popular techniques found to reduce stress derive from yoga:
    Controlled Breathing
    Meditation
    Physical Movement
    Mental Imagery

Stretching

Yoga derives its name from the word "yoke" (to bring together) and does just that by bringing together the mind, body and spirit in one practice. But whether you use yoga for spiritual transformation or for stress management and physical well-being, the benefits are numerous and include:

Reduced stress

Sound sleep

Reduced cortisol levels

Improvement of many medical conditions

Relief of allergy and asthma symptoms

Lowered blood pressure

Smoking cessation help

Lowered heart rate

Spiritual growth

Sense of well being

Reduced anxiety and muscle tension

Increased strength and flexibility

Slowed aging process

The practice of yoga involves stretching the body and forming different poses while keeping breathing slow and controlled. The body becomes relaxed and energized at the same time. There are many different styles of yoga, some moving through the poses more quickly, almost like an aerobic workout, and other styles relaxing deeply into each pose. Some have a more spiritual angle, while others are used purely as a form of exercise. Certain poses can be done just about anywhere and a yoga program can go for hours or minutes, depending on one's schedule.

HERE ARE A FEW BASICS YOGA POSTURES FOR YOU TO TRY:

Lotus Position

This is one of the meditative postures. It imitates an inverted lotus flower. The head is held erect and the eyes closed during this posture.

- Sit in a legs-crossed position with the soles of your feet turned upward and heels pressed against the lower side of your abdomen. Keep your spine straight.
- Place your hands on your knees, palms up. Hold as long as you wish.

Lotus Position

Mountain Pose

This is a basic posture of balance and control. It is the foundation for good standing posture.

- Stand in an erect position with your feet together. Press the feet flat against the floor as if to stretch them.
- Visualize a string through the spine pulling you upward, lifting the knees, hips and hamstrings.
- Equally distribute the body weight. Keep your abdomen in and chest high. Your arms may remain at your sides.

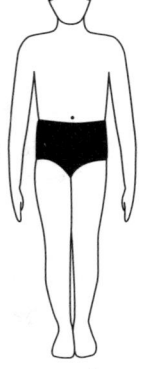

Mountain Pose

Balance Posture

This improves balance, coordination and quadriceps flexibility.

> Stand in the mountain pose. Inhale slowly and raise arm overhead.
>
> At the same time, lift your left ankle behind you and clasp it with your left hand. Shift your weight to the right side.
>
> Exhale and pull the left leg toward your body and lean forward slightly while looking forward.
>
> Your right arm will provide balance. Hold for 20 seconds. Slowly release and return to start. Repeat to opposite side.

Balance Posture

Dog and Cat Poses

This increases the flexibility of the spine and is really two poses, one flowing into the other.

> Begin on your hands and knees. Keep your hands just in front of your shoulders, your legs about hip-width apart.
>
> As you inhale, tilt the tailbone and pelvis up, and let the spine curve downward, dropping the stomach low and lift your head up. Stretch gently.

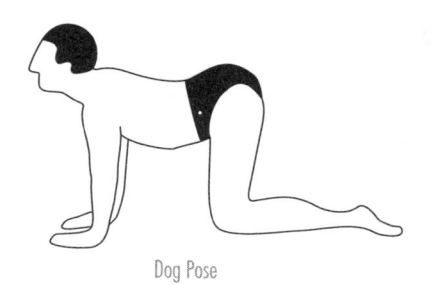

Dog Pose

As you exhale, move into cat by reversing the spinal bend, tilting the pelvis down, drawing the spine up and pulling the chest and stomach in.

Repeat several times, flowing smoothly from dog into cat, and cat back into dog.

Back Stretch

This increases spinal flexibility and strengthens the back.

Get into a seated position with legs extended forward.

Rest your hands on your thighs and straighten your spine.

Raise your arms in front of you to shoulder level.

Then proceed to raise them overhead, bending slightly backward.

Bend forward to your knees.

Grab your knees and hold the stretch for 10 seconds.

Your head should be bent forward.

Pull your body forward to your knees with the elbows bent outward. Hold for 10 seconds.

Return to upright position.

Place hands on your thighs and relax.

Back Stretch.

Simple Spinal Twist

This releases tension from the spine and promotes spinal flexibility.

Sit on the floor. Place your right sole against your left thigh.

Cross your left foot over the right knee and place the sole of your foot firmly on the floor.

Position your left hand before you.

Bring your right arm to your left knee and firmly grasp it.

Slowly twist your trunk and head to the left. Your left arm will then be placed around your waist and rested on your right side. Keep your chin close to your shoulder. Hold for 10 seconds.

Slowly move out of the posture and relax. Change leg position and repeat to other side.

Simple Spinal Twist.

Triangle Pose

This relieves tension in the neck and back.

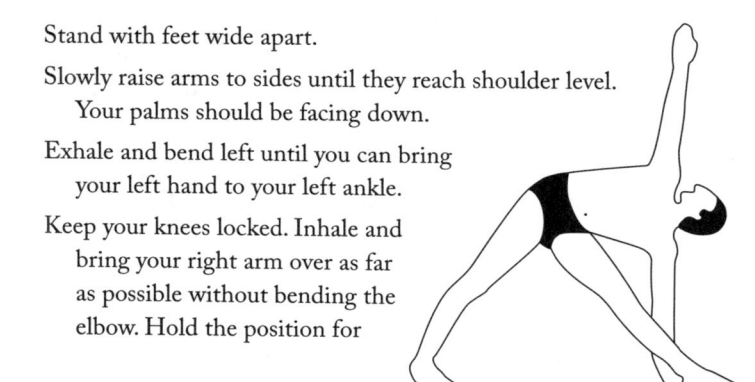

Stand with feet wide apart.

Slowly raise arms to sides until they reach shoulder level. Your palms should be facing down.

Exhale and bend left until you can bring your left hand to your left ankle.

Keep your knees locked. Inhale and bring your right arm over as far as possible without bending the elbow. Hold the position for

Triangle Pose.

20 seconds while breathing deeply and concentrating on the stretch.

Slowly straighten and return to start.

Relax for a moment and then repeat to the opposite side.

Downward Facing Dog

Builds strength, flexibility and awareness; stretches the spine and hamstrings; rests the heart.

Start on your hands and knees. Keep your legs about hip width apart and your arms shoulder width apart.

Your middle fingers should be parallel, pointing straight ahead. Roll your elbows so that the eye or inner elbow is facing forward.

Inhale and curl your toes under, as if getting ready to stand on your toes.

Exhale and straighten your legs; push upward with your arms. The goal is to lengthen the spine while keeping your legs straight and your feet flat on the ground. However, in the beginning it's okay to bend the knees a bit and to keep your heels raised.

The important thing is to work on lengthening the spine. Don't let your shoulders creep up by your ears—keep them down. Weight should be evenly distributed between your hands and feet.

Hold the position for a few breaths. Come down on and exhale. Repeat several times, synchronizing with your breath: up on the exhale and down on the inhale.

Downward Facing Dog

Shoulder Stand

This promotes circulation in chest and neck and is said to stimulate the glands, in particular the thyroid. It can also pull your neck out of alignment, so when you're done with this one, give me a call.

> Lie flat on your back.
>
> Place your hands at your sides, palms down, and begin to raise your legs. Press your hands against the floor to push your legs upward.
>
> Place your hands on hips, elbows on the ground. Try to straighten your legs and hold them upward. Your chin should be tucked in against your chest. Close your eyes and relax. Hold for 10 seconds.
>
> Bend your knees, release your hands, and slowly return to start, one vertebra at a time.

Shoulder Stand

HYDRATION FOR REDUCED STRESS

Go get a big cup or a bottle of water. Here's why:

Most of us fail to drink enough water—that's water: not tea, coffee, coke, "sports" drinks, Red Bull or fruit juice. All of your organs, including your brain, depend on water to function properly. It's just how we're built. If you starve your body of water, you'll function below your best and you will get stressed, physically and mentally.

Offices and workplaces commonly have a very dry atmosphere (due to air-conditioning and heating/ventilation systems) which increases people's susceptibility to dehydration. In this drier environment, it's even more important that you keep your body properly hydrated by regularly drinking water. Most people need four to eight glasses of water a day. You'll find it easy to drink more water if you keep some on your desk at all times – it's human nature to drink it if it's there—so go get some now!

Nature calls when you drink a lot of water, giving you a bit of a break and a bit of exercise now and then to go to the bathroom. Frequent breaks relieve stress. It's easy to see if you're properly hydrated by looking at your urine; if it's clear or near clear, you're in the clear; if it's yellow, you're not drinking enough.

You don't need to buy expensive mineral water. Tap water is fine. If you don't like the taste of tap water, it's probably because of the chlorine (aquarium fish don't like it either), however the chlorine dissipates naturally after a few hours—even through a plastic bottle—so keep some ordinary tap water in the fridge for two to three hours and try it then. If you want to be really exotic, add a slice of lemon or lime.

NUTRITION AND STRESS

Many of us eat to make ourselves feel better and often overeat. Unfortunately, most comfort foods are not good for us. Broccoli will never taste like cheesecake. So we have to have the willpower to let go of our addictions to unhealthy foods and learn to like fruits and vegetables.

Legend has it that for hundreds of thousands of years humans developed the instincts to crave sweet, fatty and salty foods in order to survive. This kept us alive through feast and famine.

Sometimes many days or even weeks would go by where there was no food to be eaten. So, thousands of years ago, these addictions kept us alive.

Nowadays, these same addictions cause chronic disease, obesity and premature death. So have an apple and learn to like it.

Each human is as different as his or her fingerprint, like a snowflake. Try different eating plans to find out which work best for you. Probably the healthiest diet is the Pritikin Eating Plan. You may want to add some low-fat protein to the program to suit it to your body's needs.

The Pritikin Eating Plan is a low-fat, mostly fruit and veggie approach developed by Nathan Pritikin in the 1950s. Fat only accounts for sixteen percent in this diet. Since 1976, more than 70,000 people have spent time at the Pritikin Longevity Centers learning how to eat healthy, prepare low-fat meals and snacks and incorporate exercise and stress-reduction techniques into their lives. In fact, the Pritikin Program was the first to demonstrate the link between diet and conquering disease. It has a long track record of reversing the leading causes of premature death in the United States and is great for losing weight.

The best part: in over 100 studies in medical journals like the New England Journal of Medicine, results have shown that the diet:

Reduces the risk factors of heart disease.

Lowers blood pressure.

Reduces key risk factors for breast, colon and prostate cancer.

The focus of the Pritikin Program is not about watching fat or carbohydrate intake. The focus is on eating healthy foods like vegetables, fruits, whole grains and low fat meats and seafood. The program also stresses the importance of including unrefined carbs, antioxidants, dietary fiber, as well as proper vitamins and minerals, while including lean meats and fatty acids. In comparison, the typical American diet tends to be high in sugar, cholesterol, refined fats and oils, sodium and "empty calories." This kind of diet puts stress on the body.

Making healthy food and diet choices is part of a healthy lifestyle. When you eat right and combine it with the exercise and relaxation techniques we've discussed in this book, you'll be well on your way to greatly reducing the stress in your life and boosting your health.

THE PRITIKIN EATING PLAN

Grains

Eat at least five servings of unrefined carbohydrates every day. This means eating whole grains (wheat, oats, rye, brown rice, barley, millet) and starchy vegetables (potatoes, yams, winter squashes, chestnuts, beans and peas). A serving is equal to approximately 1/2 cup. Work to reduce your intake of refined grains (such as white bread, white rice and pasta) to two servings per day—but avoiding these types of grains altogether is best.

Veggies

Each and every day, eat at least four vegetables, cooked or raw. A serving is about 1 cup of raw veggies or 1/2 cup of cooked veggies. I highly recommend you include dark green, yellow or orange vegetables daily. If you want to lose weight, go wild on vegetables and limit calorie-dense foods such as breads, crackers, cold cereals, fruit juices, dried fruits, nuts, seeds and refined sweeteners.

Fruits

Choose at least three fruits daily. A serving size is the size that will fit in your hand. You can substitute one serving of fruit juice (1/2 cup) daily in place of actual fruit.

Calcium-Rich Foods

Eat at least two servings of calcium-rich foods every day. You can choose nonfat milk (1 cup), nonfat yogurt (3/4 cup), nonfat ricotta (1/2 cup) or fortified and enriched nonfat or low-fat soy milk (1 cup).

Animal Proteins

Eat no more than one serving of animal protein daily. Pritikin recommends fish and shellfish over lean poultry and lean poultry over beef or pork. A serving is about 3-1/2 oz cooked or the size of the palm of your hand and the thickness of a deck of cards. Include organic or free-range beef and grass-fed bison in your diet. Eating these in small quantities can contribute to an overall healthy diet. Avoid fatty meats, organ meats and processed meats (hot dogs, bacon and bologna).

Vegetarian Options

If you're a vegetarian, you can substitute any animal protein for beans or lentils (2/3 of a cup), tofu or soy products (4-6 ounces).

Beverages

Drink lots of water, hot grain beverages (coffee substitutes), vegetable juices and herbal teas. It's important to limit caffeinated beverages to one per day. Work on replacing caffeinated beverages with decaffeinated and, if at all possible, replace coffee with tea.

FOODS TO AVOID

Salt and High Sodium Foods

Salt is in EVERYTHING nowadays—and that's not good. When you can, avoid highly-salted foods. This means avoiding pickled and smoked foods. Be sure not to exceed 1500 mg of sodium per day.

Alcohol

Most Americans drink too much. Drink in moderation or not at all. Women should limit themselves to four drinks per week. For men, the maximum recommended weekly allowance is seven drinks. Choose red wine over white wine, wine over beer and either over liquor.

Oils

Use only oils high in monounsaturated fat, such as canola, olive, avocado and peanut oils. Cut other kinds of oil out of your diet and avoid deep-fried foods. Limit oil consumption to one teaspoon per 1000 calories consumed. Avoid animal fats, tropical oils and processed or refined oils: butter, coconut oil, palm kernel oil, lard, chicken fat, palm oil, cocoa butter, margarine, hydrogenated and partially-hydrogenated vegetable oils and shortenings.

Sweeteners

Avoid sugar, fructose and high fructose corn syrup. Instead, use a maximum of two tablespoons per day of fruit juice concentrate, barley malt or rice syrup.

Miscellaneous

Avoid egg yolks, deep-fried foods, non-dairy whipped toppings, rich desserts and salty snack foods.

Like I say, this may be the best diet, especially if you add some protein to it. But it's challenging to stick with, so do your very best. Another diet that may be even healthier (but even harder to stick to) is Dr. Dean Ornish's diet. It's only ten percent fat and mostly vegetarian.

There is a health food store near my office called Larrabee Herbs, and the three nutritionists who run the place are very knowledgeable and helpful. They recommend a diet higher in protein, probably 80 grams per day. They also stress avoiding dairy, processed foods and gluten from wheat. Of course they all recommend lots of vegetables and fruits.

A lot of people have found benefits from the following eating plans, so consider one or more of the following:

1. *The South Beach Diet* by Arthur Agatston, M.D.
2. *8 Weeks to Optimal Health* by Andrew Weil, M.D.
3. *The Zone* by Barry Sears, PhD
4. Dr. Deepak Chopra's many books
5. *Fit for Life* by Harvey and Marilyn Diamond
6. *You: On a Diet: The Owner's Manual for Waist Management* by Mehmet C. Oz, M.D. and Michael F. Roizen, M.D.
7. *The Atkins Diet Plan* by Dr. Robert Atkins (I am not a fan of Atkins, but a lot of people swear by it, so who knows)

The following is a look at various herbs and their medicinal properties with regard to stress, disease and nutrition

Supplementing your diet with certain herbs can help alleviate stress. The following is a look at a few helpful herbs and their medicinal properties with regard to stress, disease and nutrition.

Astragalus: Boosts the immune system by increasing and stabilizing the white blood cell count. May help fight off colds and flu.

Echinacea: Used for centuries in the Native-American culture to stimulate the immune system, Echinacea is best known as a natural treatment for colds and flu, particularly at the onset of cold or flu-like symptoms.

Feverfew: Affects the physiological hormones that trigger migraine headaches, dramatically reducing the pain and severity.

Ginger: Known to most people as a spice for food, ginger root can also help relieve stomach cramps, motion sickness and problems associated with the gastrointestinal tract.

Ginkgo: The most popular herb taken in Europe, ginkgo is a neurostimulator. Its use is associated with increased memory function and blood flow to the brain, particularly in people over the age of 50.

Ginseng: A staple in traditional Chinese medicine, ginseng is known in the Western world as a cardiovascular enhancer.

Goldenseal: Like Echinacea, goldenseal is regarded as a natural healing agent for colds and flu.

Hawthorn Berry: Known as an anti-arrhythmia agent and used extensively in Europe to treat congestive heart failure.

Kava: Relieves anxiety and mild insomnia. Kava can also help calm you down without robbing you of alertness.

Licorice: Thought to be a good treatment for ulcer-related pain.

Milk Thistle: Known as an antitoxin, which acts like an antioxidant specifically against ailments associated with the liver.

St. Johns Wort: Widely used as a natural anti-depressant for people with mild to moderate depression.

Saw Palmetto: Alleviates problems associated with the prostate gland.

Valerian: A root extract used as a natural sedative to treat insomnia.

It's very important to note that these herbs, like standard medicine prescriptions, should only be used when needed to reestablish normal immune function or reestablish metabolic balance in the body. They are not recommended for use on an ongoing basis.

I also recommend taking a multivitamin supplement once a day for overall general health, as well as 1,000 to 3,000 mg per day of vitamin C. Emergen-C is an excellent brand.

CONCLUSION

I hope to meet you at some point, be it at one of my speeches, when I travel and present my seminars, or in my office giving you a chiropractic adjustment. My life's work is to help you achieve and maintain excellent health and help you have a happy and productive life. My work is dedicated to you enjoying your life to its fullest and having the most fun you can have, so you will like me better.

I hope this book has helped you de-stress your life and if you liked the book, let me know and if you didn't, well what do you know.

Sincerely,
Dr. Jeffrey Smith, D.C.

Email me at:
funnydr@aol.com

RECOMMENDED READING & RESOURCES

www.SageUnivesity.com

Managing Stress, by Brian L. Seaward

All books by Martin Sage

All books by Dr. Mehmet Oz, M.D. and Michael F. Roizen, M.D.

All books by Deepak Chopra, M.D.

All books by Andrew Weil, M.D.

All books by Robert Pritikin and Nathan Pritikin

All books by Dean Ornish